AN INTRODUCTION TO THE FRENCH THEATRE

By the same author

An Introduction to the Greek World
An Introduction to the Greek Theatre
Greek Scenic Conventions
Three Greek Plays for the Theatre
Plays without People: Puppetry and Serious Drama
The Theatres of Japan
The Romans and their World
Ballet of Comedians
The Byzantines and their World
The Ancient Greek and Roman Theatre

Translated by the author

Aeschylus
  Oresteia
  Prometheus Bound
  Seven Against Thebes

Sophocles
  Oedipus the King
  Antigone
  Oedipus at Colonus
  Electra

Euripides
  Hecuba
  The Madness of Heracles

Plautus
  Menaechmi
  The Pot of Gold

Aristophanes
  The Birds
  The Clouds

AN INTRODUCTION TO
THE FRENCH THEATRE

Peter D. Arnott

First published 1977 by
THE MACMILLAN PRESS LTD
London and Basingstoke
Associated companies in New York
Dublin Melbourne Johannesburg and Madras

ISBN 0 333 17647 2

Printed in Great Britain by
WESTERN PRINTING SERVICES LTD
Bristol

To Jennifer Clare
la petite récemment baptisée

Contents

Preface

Nearly twenty years ago, I wrote a short book called *An Introduction to the Greek Theatre*. It was in no sense intended as a learned work, or as a serious contribution to original scholarship. Rather, it was written out of a practitioner's enthusiasm in an attempt to do one or two very simple things: to talk about Greek plays, not as literary texts, but as *plays*, designed to be performed by actors, in a theatre, in front of an audience; and to approximate for the reader the sensation that the members of the original audience must have felt as they took their seats on the hillside, in the Greek sunshine, to watch the first performance of a work by Aeschylus, Euripides or Aristophanes some two thousand years ago. It dealt with actors, and the conditions governing their performance; with theatre structures, and the kind of environment they provided for the play; with audiences, and the willing imagination they brought with them, to allow them to serve as accomplices in the dramatic event. The book tried to sketch, also, the problems of bringing such plays to the modern spectator, given the necessity of transposing theatrical styles and conventions, and of the major difficulties inherent in the act of translation.

The present volume has the same purpose, and a substantially similar organisation. Once again, it attempts to take plays which are now more commonly read than seen, and place them in a living theatre context, sketching the environmental forces which conditioned the finished work: the shape of theatres and the texture of scenery, the pressure of critics and the response of audiences, the working habits of actors and the preconceptions of a given society. Any similarity in concept between this and the Greek book is intentional. Any difference is due to the changes that twenty years have wrought in the author. Both books have one important thing in common: they take their stand on practicality. All the plays discussed at length in the following pages are those which the author has produced, directed or acted in – even Marivaux's *Le Triomphe de Plutus*, something of a rarity in today's theatre.

To some extent the title may be considered a misnomer. This book, after all, is not an introduction to the whole of the French theatre, but only a small part of it: the period called classical or neo-classical, delimited roughly by the establishment of the Hôtel de Bourgogne as a secular playhouse in the late sixteenth century, and the fusion of the separate companies into the Comédie Française a hundred years later; the period embracing the works of Corneille and Racine in tragedy, and of Molière in comedy. This is the beginning of French drama as we know it, but in no way its sum. Where, my critic may ask, are Voltaire, Hugo, Dumas? Where are Scribe, Sardou, Feydeau? Claudel, Sartre, Cocteau, Beckett, Ionesco?

And yet, perhaps, the title is not so inappropriate after all. The influence of this period extended far beyond the death of Molière, nor did it end with the founding of the Comédie Française. Its reverberations continued to be felt. The tragic playwrights had laid down patterns which were to serve as models for generations to come, and explored areas of dramatic consciousness in ways whose influence far transcended the more obvious imitations. Let us take a few examples at random. Racine composed a kind of tragedy which refined the traditional apparatus of the theatre to its absolute minimum. His plays had simple plots framed in a sparse setting. Pageantry and spectacle, colour, fuss and noise were rejected. His characters scarcely moved, save at the most urgent and critical moments. They were left with little but their voices and their language, developed as a sublime and sensitive instrument. The Romantic drama reacted against all this – though with a vehemence which testified to the power of what it was trying to supplant – but the twentieth century has often, and in powerful ways, reaffirmed the simpler dramatic virtues. Anouilh has written an *Antigone* described as 'a text-book of tragedy', in which the physical action is minimal and the characters, kept static, do little more than debate; in which the excitement of the drama is in the thrust and riposte of argument and the clash of ideologies. Samuel Beckett, going further, has systematically stripped actors of most of their customary props and assurances. He has set them in a blasted and barely populated landscape, in which talk is the only resource; he has imprisoned them in trash cans, or buried them up to their necks in sand; he has placed them in coffins, and reduced dialogue to repetition; he has even removed language itself, writing plays in which mutes interact with inanimate objects; and, finally, has devised a drama in which the curtain rises on a bare stage, pauses for a moment, and then comes down. Ironically, the same audiences that laud Beckett's achievement as the ultimate in avant-garde theatre tend to dismiss Racine as a tedious figure from the vanished past, though both are responsive to the same principles and cherish, ultimately, a similar dramatic vision.

So it is with the comic. For instance, Jarry's ebullient, iconoclastic *Ubu Roi* seems at first sight to have little enough in common with Molière, but Jarry acknowledged an ample debt to his predecessor. Molière, he saw, had tended to reduce his major characters to a single comic impulse, a foible or obsession which governed every aspect of their lives. Jarry argued that he was simply taking this process one step further in reducing his figures to a two-dimensional cartoon-like simplicity.

The period, then, is vital, both for what it produces and for its continuing influence. For those interested in the history of the theatre, as distinct from dramatic literature, it has a further value. For all practical purposes, this is the age when we first begin to perceive actors as *people*, rather than as names on a list. What we know about Greek actors – their personalities, their training, the roles they played and their position in society – would fill little more than half a dozen pages. Information about the Romans is similarly scanty. Medieval players remain largely anonymous, as much by their own design as by the accident of history. Even for the Elizabethan age, we have little more than a handful of names which we can identify with specific roles, a few letters, and a scattering of conventional tributes. But the personnel of the seventeenth-century theatre in France we know in more detail perhaps than they would have liked. For the first time they become flesh and blood, recording powerfully and endearingly the same problems that still beset actors and actresses today. We see the squabbles, the tribulations, the professional disasters; the lack of money, the love affairs, the running wars with the critics and with Authority, in whatever form it may be vested; the rivalries, the flaring egotism, and the attempts to build a dedicated team. And as these people become more solidly known, so the period assumes a greater theatrical reality. It is no longer a collection of scripts but an assemblage of productions, with all the varied skills that this implies. It has been the intention of this book, as with its Greek predecessor, to try to flesh out the written with the human record.

My thanks are due to several people who have assisted in the preparation of this work. To Michèle Billy and Gareth Esersky, who read the manuscript at various stages; to Irene Rickabaugh, who typed it; and to Jill Silverman, who offered able assistance in the one area where I can notoriously claim no professional expertise, namely, the dance. My gratitude goes to all of them, and no less to the actors and actresses who, throughout the years, have helped me bring the plays to life.

P.D.A.

1 A Beginning, an End and a Beginning

(1) THE PLACE: UNKNOWN. THE TIME: TOWARDS THE END OF THE TWELFTH CENTURY A.D.
On a crisp spring morning, as the bells ring out, we join the growing crowd that gathers before a Norman church. All are here who can set the hours aside – nobles and villeins, farmers and their wives, merchants, travellers, clerics from the neighbouring domains – for this is a high and holy ceremony, a blazon of colour and pageantry in the drab of everyday. The doors of the church are flung wide open, and the proud, pointed arch frames humans portraying a divine action, the story of the Creation of Man, his Temptation and Fall. Within the door, dimly perceptible in the shadowed nave, stands the church choir, whose chanted Latin texts will be acted out and amplified in the vernacular by the actors. Within the doorway also sits a reader to provide appropriate scriptural passages as a linking commentary – again in Latin, for the edification of the learned and for tradition's sake. But most of the people gathered to watch the play are more interested in the actors, who will speak in good clear Norman French, to be understood. Performers and spectators alike are taking part in a common enterprise, a shared experience, whose seeds were already present in the structure of the Catholic liturgy and the symbolic action of the Mass: the process of realising the Bible story in terms of a dramatic event, with all the vividness and immediacy that this entails.

The actors appear now, as God, Adam and Eve, in the doorway. Portraying God is a priest, robed appropriately in the vestments of the Church. Adam, according to a simple colour symbolism already centuries old, is dressed in dominant red, Eve in submissive white. God recounts to them, in measured verse, the mystery of their creation, and displays the Garden of Eden which shall be their home:

> Within this garden, rich in pleasant shade,
> You will live forever, nor grow old and fade,

> And never will you suffer pain or woe.
> Here make your home, and do not seek to go.

The Earthly Paradise to which he leads them is represented by an elevated platform to the right of the church door – always, by a convention rooted in human belief and behaviour centuries before Christ was born, the lucky or the blessed side. It is draped with silken hangings that rise to shoulder height, so that once the actors are in the Garden only their upper parts are seen. This simple staging device makes the convention of stage nudity more acceptable, and at the same time gives Adam a place to hide from the wrath of God. Trees and bushes hung with fruit complete the setting, prominent among them the forbidden Tree of Knowledge:

> Eat of this fruit, wherein no perils lie,
> But from that tree alone avert thine eye,
> For if thou eat it, thou shalt surely die
> And lose my favour and goodwill thereby.

To the left of the church door, counterbalancing the Garden of Eden on the sinister, the unlucky side, is the tableau of Hell, depicted in a manner that will become increasingly familiar over centuries to come: a battlemented tower surmounting a great grinning mouth through which fantastically caparisoned devils come and go. As God leaves his creations to enjoy the Earthly Paradise, Hell's denizens appear, scampering through the audience and gradually approaching Adam to entice him to eat the forbidden fruit. If he does, they promise:

> Straightway your eyes shall opened be
> All the future for to see.
> All things shall be at your command
> If on this fruit you set your hand.
> Eat, for it will profit you
> And of God make no ado,
> For his equal you shall be.

Adam resists, but Eve proves more susceptible to flattery:

> For you were never made hard blows to bear,
> You are more tender than the rose is fair,
> Your face with clearer light than crystal glows,
> Or ice beneath a canopy of snows.

Eve succumbs and tempts Adam to eat. The fatal act is watched by a mechanical serpent drawn by some device into the branches of the tree. Now the familiar consequences ensue. Conscious of their sin, Adam and Eve dive out of sight and emerge in a change of costume, being now wrapped in garments of fig leaves. Accusing and counteraccusing each other, they are driven from Eden by God and an angel vested in white. The divine personages retire into the church. There follows an elaborate mime scene in which Adam and Eve, now condemned to toil for their food, go through the motions of tilling and planting the soil, only to be frustrated by the devils who reappear maliciously from Hell to sow thorns among the crops. In a prolonged fit of lamentation Adam and Eve fall to the ground, bewailing their error and their hard lot. As they cry, the devils surround them. Throwing iron collars about their necks, and leaping and dancing for joy, they drag them away to perdition. As they pass through Hellmouth a cloud of smoke belches forth, and unseen stagehands set up a prodigious clattering of pots and pans.

(2) THE PLACE: BOURGES. THE TIME: SPRING 1536

Open a map of France and put your finger on the centre of the country; it will fall not far from Bourges. Built on a hill, the city overlooks the streams that flow into the Cher, and so to the Loire and the sea. Julius Caesar, when he conquered the Gauls, noted it as one of the most beautiful sites of his new province. Roman occupation left its familiar mark in the shape of public buildings, which remained in view, and sometimes in use, when France reacquired its independence. During the Middle Ages Bourges added a magnificent cathedral and a scattering of great houses. It held a university and school of law which were internationally famous. It was a trading town, whose merchants grew numerous and prospered; and it produced several powerful individuals whose names were to be written large in the history of France.

By this time, more than three hundred years after the appearance of our Norman drama, the production of religious plays had become ingrained in the pattern of French urban life. A number of cities now offered such spectacles on a regular basis. They were beloved by the Church, as offering a picturesque and effective means of indoctrination; they were popular with the merchants who now helped sponsor them, because they attracted crowds of tourists who were good for trade, and offered a rich chance of financial profit; and, finally, they were no less popular with the citizens who watched them and performed in them, because they grew continually more lavish, colourful and exciting and afforded a legitimate respite from more humdrum duties. But popular demand had distorted the product. The scripts were now complicated beyond anything the author of the *Play of Adam* could have dreamed of. Their scope had expanded to embrace material from the Old and New Testaments, the gaudier episodes of the Apocrypha and the folk-lore of the saints. Nor was this the only aspect in which the earlier simplicity and innocence had been lost. The productions of these religious extravaganzas were now vast community enterprises, demanding astute financial management, professional writing and direction, and public involvement to an unparalleled degree. It was to just such a production, inspired by a similar event in the city's neighbour town of Issoudun, that the people of Bourges directed their efforts in 1536.

All segments of the population were represented. The backers were men of commercial and social repute and the actors drawn from the community at large. Members of the clergy, relishing their special dispensations, abandoned their customary offices to play the principal sacred roles, while students, merchants and artisans filled out the rest of the enormous cast. Splendid costumes were made locally, at great expense, and the city's own historic past provided a suitable location for the performance in the remains of a Roman amphitheatre originally located outside the city limits but now embraced within the medieval walls. In 1536 this was refurbished, and fitted out with tiers of galleries much in the Roman manner. The playing space, arranged perhaps arena style, perhaps more probably in the half-round, gave ample room for the variety and mechanical complexity of the settings that this sprawling, overblown play needed.

The festivities began on the last day of April with a solemn Mass, followed by a procession in which both the civic authorities and the performers joined. Marching to the sound of fife and drum they wound their way from the abbey through the tangle of streets towards the theatre. All the players wore their costumes. Here were the Apostles in contrasting colours, Peter in crimson and Thomas in tan, a purple Matthew and a blue Saint John; here was the Virgin Mary, blue-skirted according to tradition and bonneted with gold, and Satan in a shaggy velvet coat with a serpent for a belt and other snakes hung round about him. Here were other princes of Hell, shooting off flames and fireworks to delight the crowd. And here was Hell itself, on a cart, made in the form of a blazing tower mounted on a rock which crawled with toads and serpents. From the summit of the tower rose the head and shoulders of Lucifer, who spat fire from his muzzle and contemplated the agonies of souls in torment. There was a cart representing Heaven too, hung about with pasteboard clouds and effigies of enthroned angels, with the

Holy Trinity in glory at the centre of the tableau. Here was a dragon, with wings; here was the Emperor Nero attended by blackamoors; here were characters drawn from fact and fancy, from legend, Bible and Apocrypha, dressed in every rich fabric that an important textile city could provide, and adorned with every extravagance that religious symbolism could suggest, or the imagination of artist and maskmaker engender.

Drawn up in the amphitheatre, the Hell and Heaven wagons framed the action, with other structures moving into place between them as the long and diverse drama dictated. The play's ostensible subject was the Acts of the Apostles; it pursued the spread of God's word throughout the nations in elaborate, circumstantial and often irrelevant detail. Much attention was given to St Etienne, the patron saint of Bourges, who had been stoned to death by the Romans. A large part of the story was devoted to St Paul, whose persecution of the Christians and subsequent conversion on the road to Damascus were depicted. There followed scenes of his missionary journeys by sea, in a miniature boat which sailed on real water and capsized on cue. The audience was regaled with the stoning of Matthias and the flaying of Bartholomew; with the contest of miracles between St Peter and Simon Magus; with stage fires and earthquakes, pyrotechnic lightning and thunder, heads and hands cut off and bowels ripped out – effects sometimes merely suggested, but more often depicted with that scrupulous detail and macabre mechanical invention for which medieval stage managers were well known.

It is a matter of sad record that this great spectacle fell short of its hoped-for success. Perhaps the performance was truncated because of public indifference, religious controversy or the current war-scare; perhaps the audience, already sated with stage blood and guts in the name of religion, had grown blasé. At any rate, some of the backers lost money, and the following year a number of the masks and figures that had been constructed for the performance were sold off; the experiment was not to be repeated at Bourges. None the less, the surviving records give a clear idea of the magnificence of the attempt, and of the complex organism that the French religious drama had become.

(3) THE PLACE: PARIS. THE TIME: 1536–1548.
Of course the capital was not to be outdone by the provinces. Like other cities, Paris had its own religious plays, and here, as elsewhere, they were presented by associations created for the purpose. One group that achieved particular prominence was the Confrérie de la Passion. Formed some time in the latter part of the fourteenth century, this company

makes its first appearance in recorded history in June 1398, playing at Saint-Maur, near Vincennes. Faced with magisterial disapproval of their playing sacred dramas in the capital, the members of the Confrérie sought royal protection, perhaps with greater success than they could have hoped. In December 1402 they were granted letters patent by Charles VI, which awarded them not merely the right to play in Paris, but the virtual monopoly of all religious drama there. Their first Paris theatre was the great hall of the Hospital of the Trinity; near the Porte St Denis. Here they played scenes from the New Testament, which as time went by followed the common pattern of medieval drama in adding more and more secular material. Popular farces offered light relief from the religious plays, and as the sacred impulse waned and theatrical tastes grew less austere, it was increasingly this kind of material that audiences came to see.

The Hospital of the Trinity remained the home of the Confrérie for 137 years. What was performed during this period we do not always know. Our knowledge of the medieval French theatre presents the same tantalising gaps as the English. Though we often know, in considerable detail, what was going on in the provinces, we are usually left with only the vaguest notion of what was happening in the capital. The anticlerical purges of the Revolution in France, and the Protestant Reformation in England, must have obliterated many records of the early church that we should dearly love to have. We do know that between 1450 and 1540 the Confrérie gave at least seven performances in Paris of one of the most famous religious dramas of its time, Greban's *Passion*. We know, too, that its amateur actors were paying annual visits to Rouen, a city which had in earlier days presented a sumptuous production of its own, and which was later to gain new importance in French theatrical history as the home of Corneille.

The sixteenth century brought changes. With its charter reaffirmed by François I in 1518, the company looked about for new lodgings. In 1539 suitable premises were found in the Hôtel de Flandres, one of the big town houses built for an earlier era and now ruinous and deserted; it was only one of fourteen such faded mansions put up for sale in the same year, and probably scheduled for demolition even as the company moved in, for it was pulled down in 1543. During its short tenancy, however, the Confrérie played the *Passion* in its great hall, hung for the occasion with tapestries and fitted out with scaffolds for the audience; the performance was honoured by the presence of the King.

At the end of 1540 the Confrérie decided to break away from its usual repertoire and offer something new for Paris, the same *Acts of the*

Apostles that had been given a few years previously at Bourges. No doubt there was some jealousy here; it was inappropriate that so sumptuous a work should be left to the provinces. Also, the *Acts of the Apostles* would provide a sequel to the company's usual offering.

Like similar fraternities elsewhere, the Confrérie de la Passion was an association of merchants, tradesmen and representatives of the professions, governed at this time by a committee of four: an upholsterer, a butcher, a florist, and a barrister. Their directives went out, the forthcoming production was publicised, negotiations took place over rights to the text (with the Confrérie standing firm on its monopoly in Paris) and parts were assigned. Nervous, perhaps, about continuing to perform in a building that might shortly tumble about their ears, the brethren issued an appeal in verse to the King, asking him to provide them with a permanent theatre. It should be built in the Roman style, dedicated to the glory of the royal name and the encouragement of virtue:

> The Roman Scaurus as your model take,
> Who once, when aedile, did for Sulla make
> A theatre, that architects contrived
> And many Latin writers have described.

Is this simply the flower of oratory, or did they seriously contemplate constructing a neo-Roman theatre in Paris to outdo the genuine amphitheatre at Bourges? It was a time when such classical explorations were in the air, and Italy was producing its Renaissance recreations of Roman theatres. We do not know; nor are we even sure if, when the performance was eventually given – in the same Hôtel de Flandres, for the petition failed – it was indoors or outdoors. A contemporary account describes a theatre-in-the-round, *à la romaine*, with twenty tiers of seats and covered with awnings; and the May climate, when the *Acts of the Apostles* was given, would have made an alfresco theatre feasible. Or was the 'Roman' theatre built indoors, under the safety of a roof, as at Vicenza?

In any case, the performance was a great success. It ran for a total of thirty-five days, not, of course continuously, but spread over six months on Sundays, saints' days and holidays. The people of Paris swarmed to it, to such an extent that church services often had to be cancelled for lack of a congregation. Even the nobility attended, and the reaction was one of general delight.

But this was the swan-song of the Confrérie de la Passion in its old form. By 1542, the public temper had changed. In that year, when the

brethren announced that they would play the *Mystery of the Old
Testament*, they were met with a stinging rebuke from a *procureur
général* of the Parliament of Paris:

> The producers and actors alike are uneducated people, artisans and
> manual labourers who have never learnt their ABC; who have never
> had any training or public instruction in the giving of such per-
> formances; and who, moreover, are so uncouth in speech, lacking in
> vocabulary and faulty in pronunciation that they will often split one
> word into three, pause or break the sentence in the middle of a clause,
> make an exclamation out of what should be a question, or use some
> emphasis, gesture or accent which runs counter to the sense. This
> customarily provokes public ridicule, and creates such an uproar
> within the walls of the theatre that the play, far from edifying the
> audience, turns into a mockery and a public scandal.

Beneath the dry lawyer's language we detect a changing temper, and
the end of an age. A few years later, the Confrérie was explicitly forbidden to handle religious material, and a tradition of centuries ignobly
expired. Thus ended, for all practical purposes, the amateur performance
of sacred drama in France. The end came about not, as in England,
because of religious controversy and a desire to expel old doctrines, but
because a mode of performance had reached its natural term, grown
weary and passed away. Yet from the demolition of the old repertoire
arose the seeds of the new. The Confrérie itself did not pass away. On
the contrary, it took on a new guise and a number of years of hearty
life, in which it was to make a major impact on a new kind of theatre
for a new age.

2 Paris and its Theatres

In the winter of 1972-3, the Comédie Française, the National Theatre of France, fell victim to a stagehands' strike and could no longer operate in its usual premises. A temporary move was made to the Tuileries Gardens, where the company played under canvas. For a theatre which had always been mindful of its own past, this disruption must have prompted ironic comparisons with its earliest beginnings, and the way in which the first professional companies had to struggle not merely for a public but for a precarious footing on Parisian soil. As permanent, professional companies assembled from the debris of the amateur, sacred drama, touring became a fact of life. The actors' travels took them far afield, through France and the adjacent countries, under the passing patronage of princes both native and foreign. Thus, for instance, Valleran le Conte stumped through the provinces obstinately touting the plays of Alexandre Hardy; and for him, as for others, Paris, the centre of things, the place where everyone desired to be, proved the hardest nut to crack. It took a long time for the professional drama to establish itself as worthy of serious literary and critical interest. It took even longer for professional companies to establish themselves as a permanent feature of the urban scene, working in their own playhouses and free from threat of eviction and disturbance. A number of reasons have been suggested for this, not least the smouldering hostility of powerful segments of the Church. These will be considered in more detail later. It seems equally true, however, that at least initially, the actors' chief enemy was public indifference. People did not particularly want to see plays. Nor did they want actors located in their own community. One of the invariable laws of the theatre applies: that while amateur acting, in all countries and at all periods, has been considered totally respectable, the shift to professionalism brings a stigma and a sharp decline in social status. As the Greek actors of the fourth century B.C. had found, and the Romans after them; as the Elizabethan players had discovered when, the better part of a century before, they had made the same transition; to attempt to earn money by performing roles in public is automatically to incur the suspicion and the outright hostility of the populace. In the French theatre, as in the English, it eventually took royal patronage to transform these makeshift beginnings into permanent playhouses with the assurance of funds and public support.

In the second half of the sixteenth century Paris was still a medieval city. It was still cramped within its defensive walls, though here and there the pressures of urban living forced extrusions beyond. Its streets were narrow, pestilent and unsafe. It was grossly overcrowded, holding perhaps half a million people in its centre and as many again in the outskirts and the *faubourgs* outside the walls. But in urban planning, as in drama, this was a period of change. The reconstruction of Paris was begun in 1594 by Henri IV, continued by Louis XIII and his minister Richelieu, and brought to a peak by Louis XIV. This was the time when the city acquired many of its now famous landmarks – not, of course, the *grands boulevards*, which were to come much later, but bridges and squares. In the centre of the Seine was the Ile de la Cité, the capital's primitive heart, where the first settlers had built their wattle huts long before the Roman invaders came. Already graced with the Cathedral of Nôtre Dame, it now began to bloom with other splendid buildings both private and public. The smaller islands of the Seine were joined; they became densely populated, and highly fashionable. Henri IV added the Place Dauphine, and completed the Pont Neuf joining the Ile de la Cité to the Right Bank – a bridge designed to be free of the medieval encumbrance of houses, and to permit an easy flow of traffic. At one end stood the waterpump and fountain adorned with sculptures of Christ and the Woman of Samaria, which defeated the architect's purpose by becoming a place of popular resort. People loved to stop and gossip there, and the street hawkers discovered a new place of trade. Appropriately, the site is now marked by the giant department store of La Samaritaine.

On the Right Bank, long established as the fashionable side, the principal building was the Palace of the Louvre. This too underwent considerable enlargement and renovation. Henri IV threw out the Great Gallery to connect with the Tuileries down river. Louis XIII added the Pavillon de l'Horloge. Louis XIV, though he used the Louvre, cordially disliked it, and preferred to establish himself elsewhere. But the Louvre's chief interest for us, throughout the period, is that it contained several halls which could be used for the performance of plays. As royal interest in the drama increased, these were made available on a temporary or permanent basis to various companies.

One of these was the Salle du Petit-Bourbon, adjacent to the royal

quarters. It was a huge hall. Translating the archaic French measure-
ments of *toise*, *pied* and *pas commun*, one arrives at approximate
dimensions of 45′ × 221′, with a ceiling compared in height to the
churches of St Germain and St Eustache. Along each side ran two tiers
of galleries, partitioned into boxes, or *loges*. It functioned principally as
a conference hall, and could hold the assembly of the États-generaux
with ease. It was useful for balls and for the court ballet, where mass
movement and complicated scenic tableaux demanded a good deal of
floorspace. For the same reason it was also happily suited to the elaborate
apparatus of the 'machine plays' which became fashionable during the
period. It was here that Corneille's *Andromède*, which established the
vogue, opened after several postponements in 1650, and the audience
saw a prologue in which 'high in the air on one side there appears the
rising Sun, in a luminous chariot drawn by the four horses attributed to
him by Ovid; and on the other, on a mountaintop, the Muse of Tragedy,
who borrows his rays to illumine the theatre she has prepared for the
King's diversion'. Though ideal for such sumptuous effects, the Petit-
Bourbon was less comfortable with the legitimate drama. It was briefly
occupied by Molière's company on its return to Paris in 1658, only to be
torn down, almost literally over the actors' heads, soon afterwards in
one of the periodic spasms of palace reconstruction.

Another, slightly smaller, hall was the Salle des Gardes du Vieux
Louvre, used chiefly for assemblies and occasionally for plays. This may
have been the site of the famous royal command performance that en-
sured Molière's entrée into Paris. Also within the palace complex was
the notable Salle des Machines, designed and begun by the Italian
Vigarani, and a spectacle in itself. This had seating in the manner of a
Roman amphitheatre, with the addition of galleries two rows deep,
looking down on a stage with the extraordinary depth of 132′ specially
constructed for massive mechanical spectacle. But the acoustics were
poor, and the theatre was little used after the 1660s. When it finally
burned down, a whole new theatre, auditorium and all, was erected in
the space originally used for the stage alone.

Across the road from the Louvre, Cardinal Richelieu sought immor-
tality with his own building programme. Previous to this he had often
staged plays on the other side of Paris in the Arsénale, a complex of
halls, malls and gardens near the fashionable Place Royale. Now he
shifted his interest to the palace district, extending the ancient fortifica-
tions westward to encompass a new 'Quarter Richelieu' and the Palais
Cardinal. This contained two theatres. The smaller, holding six hundred
spectators, was used for a number of private and amateur performances,

including a famous parody of *Le Cid* in 1637. The larger Théâtre du Palais Cardinal (continuing as the Palais Royal after Richelieu's bequest to the King) held perhaps five times this number. Molière moved here after the debacle of the Petit-Bourbon, taking with him the seats he had salvaged from the wreck. By the early 1670s, although accurate reconstruction is impossible, it had clearly developed into a large and complex building offering the maximum range of seating on all levels and comfortable stage space.

But these were special theatres, dispensed by royal patronage and designed particularly for a kind of performance that was itself a lavish outgrowth of court ceremony. The workaday actor could expect less commodious quarters in less fashionable districts. While the royal houses conferred prestige, the greatest influence on the theatrical century came from humbler sources. To trace these we must leave the court for the market-place and return to the Confrérie de la Passion whose career we abandoned at a low ebb.

Some way north of the Louvre was the district later to be described as *le ventre de Paris*, the great central market. Originally this had been an open area; in the twelfth century Louis VI set aside some fields for the purpose, and the surrounding streets began to acquire appropriate names – the *rue de la Fromagerie*, Cheesemongers' Lane; the *rue de la Cordonnerie*, Rope Walk, Philippe-Auguste built a corn exchange, the Halle au Blé. Louis IX added covered fishmarkets. By the early seventeenth century the area had developed into a market for all kinds of goods known universally as Les Halles. Where the markets were the people congregated and street entertainment, of one sort or another, thrived. Here stood the famous revolving pillory where crowds assembled to mock and pelt the prisoners, and strolling players found the market a natural home. Molière was born nearby, and it is likely that his first contact with the theatre was the sight of these fly-by-night entertainers bellowing their coarse jokes from a rickety trestle stage. The history of Les Halles is substantially that of London's Covent Garden, with the market at the heart and the theatres growing up on the fringes. In both cities, in our time, the market has departed, but in Paris at least, though the traders have been wafted out to Orly, something of the old tradition remains. In the skeletons of the remaining market halls, preserved from demolition by massive, outraged public protest, café theatres and satirical cabarets still draw an audience. The popular theatre of yesterday has become today's avant-garde.

Two blocks north of Les Halles stood a building with a long history of its own. This was the Hôtel de Bourgogne, originally constructed as the town residence of the Dukes of Burgundy. Hôtel, of course, does not mean hotel. An English visitor of the eighteenth century expressed surprise that the French should give to a private house a title reserved by the English for a place of public lodging. But he could have found parallels for this semantic confusion in his own language: in the middle ages 'inn' was regularly used for a large private house with ample accommodation for personal guests. Like many of the older Paris mansions, the Hôtel de Bourgogne fell into decay, and on 11 October 1543 François I ordered this and other dilapidated properties to be put up for sale by auction. Part of the land was bought by a merchant, Jean Rouvet, with an eye to redevelopment; but shortly afterwards rather more than half the lot was resold to the Confrérie de la Passion, which was once again in search of new quarters. The Confrérie declared its intention of building a new hall for the performance of plays.

But what plays? Here the brethren seem to have been motivated by an optimism unjustified by the facts. They decorated their new hall, which went up rapidly, with the symbols of Christ's Passion, presumably assuming, in spite of the strictures against them, that they could continue with their traditional repertoire. But this was now snatched from them. On 17 November 1548 the Parliament of Paris banned the performance of sacred mysteries in the new hall – and thus, by definition, anywhere in Paris, since the Confrérie held the monopoly. By way of compensation, the new theatre could be used for 'secular mysteries' as long as these were 'honourable and legitimate'; and no play was to be permitted in Paris except under the auspices of the Confrérie.

The Confrérie had thus at one blow lost a past and gained a future. The material benefits of the new dispensation were quickly realised. With their monopoly reaffirmed by a succession of rulers, the brethren secured a stranglehold on theatrical development in Paris which only time, laborious legal process and royal intervention could break. The Confrérie was now entitled to create its own troupe, operating on its own premises, or to rent out those premises to others with total freedom from competition. Companies wishing to play elsewhere in Paris could do so only by payment of a substantial fee to the Confrérie. Inevitably, this authority was resented, and the following years reveal a sordid history of protest and litigation. Enemies of the Hôtel de Bourgogne claimed that it was unfaithful to the terms of its charter, and performed material which could hardly be called 'honourable and legitimate.' In 1588 we read:

In this place are enacted scandalous love-affairs by the hundred, a threat to the purity and morals of our womenfolk and the ruin of the poor working classes who crowd the pit, arriving two hours or more before the play begins and frittering their time away in lewdness and profanity, with games of cards and dice, with gluttony and drunkenness ... which often erupt into quarrels and brawls.

Another grievance was the Confrérie's insistence, even when the theatre was leased out, on retaining blocks of seats for its own use. This too had to be fought out by litigation and petitions to the King. And worst of all was the Confrérie's jealous protection of its own privileges, which caused it to look askance even on the amateur performance of plays, and to inflict punitive fines on anyone ignoring the monopoly.

What did the Hôtel de Bourgogne look like? The question is important, because the shape of the theatre tends to dictate the shape of the play, and many characteristic features of the French drama can be traced to the physical environment in which the works were performed. In the case of this theatre, the answer was for long uncertain. We know its location, at the corner of the rue Mauconseil and the rue Saint François (now the rue Française.) We know the size of the original parcel of land purchased by the Confrérie, and how this was reduced by subdivision. We have contemporary street-maps of Paris which show the approximate shape of the building. We have illustrations which purport to show its appearance from the street, though these are clumsily drawn and less than flattering; the Hôtel de Bourgogne appears as a squat, lumpish building, as undistinguished in architecture as it was distinguished in reputation. None of these sources provides definitive information. Over the years, however, scholars have painstakingly reconstructed the probable dimensions. Contemporary building practices, builders' contracts, standard timber sizes, title deeds, seating records, have each contributed a mite of information which leads to a plausible restoration of the whole.

It now appears that, after the subdivision of the lot, the Confrérie was left with an L-shaped parcel of land on which to build. The main rectangle was used for the theatre proper, with the projection serving as a small courtyard with a gallery and an additional small building, used perhaps for actors' lodgings or scene storage. The theatre itself was long and narrow, 17 × 7 *toises*, or approximately 107′ × 44′. Over half the floor space was taken up by the *parterre* (pit), in which there was no fixed seating, though stools and benches could be brought in. Behind the *parterre* rose the *amphithéâtre*, a bank of steeply tiered seats offering rather cramped accommodation. Overhanging these were at least two

tiers of boxes, *loges*; in each tier there were seven *loges* down the long
sides of the theatre and five facing the stage. Above these may have been
yet another tier, the *paradis* or 'gods'.

This left little room for the stage. Allowing for supporting columns,
the proscenium opening cannot have been more than 5 *toises* wide
(approximately 30'). The stage was pushed forward during a rebuilding
in 1647, but earlier than this, during the most influential period of the
theatre's development (and the period for which, incidentally, we have
a number of set designs) the space available to actors was about 4 *toises*
(25') square. Not impossible, but certainly cramped by modern standards,
which would ask another ten feet as a desirable minimum; and illuminating by comparison with the royal theatres previously described. During
the seventeenth century a number of productions created for royal fêtes
and galas were transferred to commercial houses, which must have led
to many an awkward reappraisal of set designs and stage machinery.

We may colour this statistical reconstruction of the Hôtel de Bourgogne with an imaginative one. Rostand's *Cyrano de Bergerac* (1897)
has its opening scenes set in the Hôtel in 1640. With a long stage
direction and a series of delightful vignettes, Rostand evokes a typical
pre-performance atmosphere. The proscenium is curtained off with
tapestry, and decorated with a motif of Harlequin's cloak combined with
the royal arms. A buffet stands in the auditorium, with bottles, glasses
and cakes set out for sale to the patrons. Red posters, the traditional
colour of the Bourgogne, announce the current attraction. In the middle
of the *parterre* chandeliers are lowered close to the floor, waiting to be
lit. Slowly the public begins to arrive: gentlemen, tradesmen, lackeys,
pages, pickpockets, an orange girl. A guardsman squabbles with the
doorkeeper, insisting that as a member of the Royal Household he has a
right to be admitted free. Two others fence to pass the time. A game of
cards begins. Someone has brought his lunch. A group of pages enters
in holiday mood, singing and dancing. Impatient voices call for the
candles to be lit. The gentry saunter in, the chandeliers soar to the
ceiling, the statutory three knocks are sounded and the play begins.

The Hôtel de Bourgogne survived as an independent institution for
most of the century. When the various troupes were finally merged to
form the nucleus of the National Theatre, the old building gradually
fell into disuse. It held an Italian troupe for a while, then closed for
nineteen years; it reopened in 1716, was closed in 1782, and fell to the
wreckers in the year following, with a warehouse for leather goods
occupying the old site. Hardly any trace of it remains. Just as Shakespeare's Globe has been covered by a brewery, so the remnants of the

Hôtel de Bourgogne lie at a busy Paris junction submerged under concrete. Only one broken tower of the Duke of Burgundy's original property may still be seen. But in its prime the Hôtel, for better or worse, set its stamp on the age. Even after its rivals were legitimately established, it continued to vaunt its claim as the only true royal theatre. Its actors were *les comédiens de l'élite royale* and established a distinctive style which was to colour the French theatre for centuries to come. Authors basked in its prestige. Its rivals might resent it, parody it or react against it. They could never ignore it.

The first serious commercial opposition to the Hôtel de Bourgogne arose to the north-east, in a quarter very different in character from Les Halles but still an easy walk from the senior theatre. This was the district known as *le Marais* 'the marsh', waterlogged land within the city walls which had gradually been reclaimed for residential use. About 1180 it acquired its first distinction when the Order of Knights Templar of Jerusalem, founded out of the Crusades to protect the Holy Places, established a headquarters there, just as they did in London. The street names and the Temple Métro station still recall this foundation; and, coincidentally, both the Paris and the London Temples acquired theatres in the neighbourhood. In Paris, fashion moved in where the Templars had led. Systematically the marshes were drained – the windmills and canals feature prominently on contemporary maps – and the Marais turned into an aristocratic quarter. Even in the turmoil of modern Paris it still retains an air of faded dignity, with streets of aloof old houses often possessing fascinating individual histories.

In this unlikely district there arrived, in 1629, a company from Rouen, which we have already noted as a city with strong theatrical connections. Its leader was Guillaume Desgilberts, better known under his stage name as Montdory. Its principal playwright was Rouen's own Pierre Corneille. Montdory had served his apprenticeship in barnstorming. He had been the pupil of Valleran le Conte, worked in the troupe of the Prince of Orange, and headed his own company in the provinces. Now he dared to establish himself in Paris and challenge the monopoly of the Bourgogne on its own ground.

There is a common pattern in the history of the theatre: plays, as a rule, come before buildings. The first companies, performing only sporadically or moving from place to place on tour, find no structures specially conceived to house their works for the professional theatre building does not yet exist. They therefore occupy any existing building which happens to be roughly suitable, and adapt it to their needs. There are certain minimum requirements. Is there space for a sufficient audience? Can the entrance of this audience be controlled, particularly with a view to taking admission money? Can the performers find a focal point to ensure that they will be seen? – which almost invariably involves mounting themselves on a platform which they carry with them. It is possible to see the whole history of theatre architecture as deriving from a combination of these two factors, a platform for the actors to stand on, and the kind of space locally available in which they can set it. In Greece, the players of Thespis erect their platform on the rim of the village threshing floor and originate the distinctive circular form, with its scene-building appendage, of the Greek theatre. In Spain the platform is raised in the square formed by the backs of houses, and produces the *corral*. In Tudor England, the platform set in a galleried innyard or banquet hall evolves into the characteristic upper and lower acting levels of the Elizabethan public playhouse. In Japan, the platform set among the typical buildings of the Buddhist shrine begets the *noh* stage. The use of such temporary buildings conditions stage decoration and actors' behaviour. When, in the course of time, the drama has acquired sufficient permanency and stature to deserve buildings of its own, these buildings continue to embody the practices enforced by the temporary structures.

Thus in Paris, when the Confrérie finally constructed its own house, the design was undoubtedly influenced by the various halls and other spaces that the group had inhabited in the past. Even the concept of the *amphithéâtre* seems to owe something to the outdoor performances of the Middle Ages. Similarly, when Montdory's company settled in the capital, it located itself in a type of building that was probably familiar from touring days, and that eventually produced a characteristic French theatre shape. This was a tennis court – not, of course, lawn tennis, for this modern game did not burst upon the world until the 1870s, but the indoor game known variously as royal or court tennis and in French as the *jeu de paume*. Its origins reach back at least as far as Greek antiquity, and by the fourteenth century it was already a favourite sport of French kings. In Shakespeare's *Henry V*, when the Dauphin insults the English ruler with a gift of tennis balls, it is this game that he has in mind. By the end of the sixteenth century there were said to be 250 such courts in Paris alone. In England one of the most famous examples, which still survives, was built by Henry VIII for his palace at Hampton Court, and though the game has largely died out, a few structures of more recent vintage are still in regular use.

The royal tennis court had a distinctive but adaptable design. It was a long narrow building (modern dimensions are approximately 110′ × 38′)

with most of the floorspace taken up by the court itself. Down one long side, and later along both short sides as well, ran a low roofed gallery. A rope or net divided the court, as in lawn tennis, but the game itself was considerably more complicated than its modern successor. Special areas were marked out on the floor and walls, and the player could gain points by hitting targets at either end. Windows mounted high in the walls for safety's sake provided illumination.

The theatrical possibilities of such a structure are obvious. With a stage and proscenium erected at one end, the bulk of the floorspace could be used as the *parterre*. Either the existing architecture of the covered galleries could be utilised or, with some extra trouble, *loges* could be erected round the walls. This history of French companies at this period shows the comparative ease with which such modifications could be made, or disassembled for transportation to another site. A tennis court could thus be taken over permanently as a theatre, particularly since, during the seventeenth century, the popularity of the game seems to have been on the wane, or, if it profited the proprietor, serve a double function. Often, too, the tennis court may have had subsidiary buildings that the actors could use. At Hampton Court there is an adjacent suite of changing rooms, and this must have been true of some of the larger French examples also. The fashion of transforming a tennis court into a theatre is not confined to France, but appears in England at this period also. When the restoration of Charles II in 1660 made it possible for the theatres to resume their legal existence after the Puritan interregnum, the London companies found most of the old public playhouses destroyed, decayed or unusable. They promptly followed the French precedent, and Lyle's and Gibbon's tennis courts enjoyed a new lease of life. As late as 1695 we find Congreve's *Love for Love* opening in such a place, with an appropriate reference in the Epilogue:

> And thus, our audience, which did once resort
> To shining theatres to see our sport,
> Now find us tossed into a tennis court.
> These walls but t'other day were filled with noise
> Of roaring gamesters, and your damn-me boys;
> Then bounding balls and rackets they encompast,
> And now they're filled with jests, and flights, and bombast!

To return to Montdory's actors, such was the home they found in Paris, though there was some difficulty in settling permanently. For the first few years they jumped from one tennis court to another within the

Marais quarter. These were not easy years. They were dogged by the malevolence of the Hôtel de Bourgogne, which insisted on its monopoly and demanded its money. The new company made its name with Corneille's *Mélite*, a supposedly autobiographical comedy based on a love-affair of the author, but composed in a new, economical mode. Though it got off to a slow start it grew into a huge popular success. Corneille later wrote smugly:

> The success of this play was astonishing. It established a new theatre company in Paris, in defiance of the troupe which claimed to be the one and only. It was as good as anything that had been written up to that time, and made my name at court. The common sense which is my constant guide led me to devise a unity of action by involving four lovers in a single plot, and gave me such repugnance for the barbaric practice of displaying Paris, Rome and Constantinople on the same stage that I compressed the location of my play into one city.

This same success, however, left the company facing a fine of three crowns a day for a total of 135 performances, demanded by the Hôtel de Bourgogne and upheld by the justices. Montdory also had to contend with the hostility of his neighbours, who complained that their quiet streets were becoming jammed with traffic – a clear tribute to the new company's popularity. This kind of protest continues through the century. Though people were increasingly inclined to accept the theatre in the abstract, they were less happy about having it – even the Hôtel de Bourgogne – on their doorsteps.

At the beginning of 1634 the company moved to its fourth and final home, the *jeu de paume des Marais*, today 90, rue Vieille du Temple. Prepared now to gamble on its legal future, it paid a high rent for a long lease. There were five male members of the company besides Montdory, and two actresses. In an age when husband-and-wife acting teams were the rule, Montdory's wife was unusual in that she never set foot on stage; she was 'an innocent, who never sticks her head outside the church door'. Corneille provided the repertory, with a succession of smart social comedies in fashionable Paris settings. Audiences felt they could identify with *La Galérie du Palais*, and needed only to step outdoors to sample the real life of *La Place Royale*. Corneille's critics accused him of only pretending to borrow local colour, and sneered that he was using Paris place-names as a publicity device; they looked forward sarcastically to the day when he would give them *The St. Jean Cemetery*, *La Samaritaine* and *The Cattle Market*. But the public came in crowds and influential backers followed, eventually including Richelieu himself. The company found itself invited to give royal command performances. It was awarded the title of *la Troupe du Roi au Marais* and, starting in 1635, an annual subsidy of 6000 *livres*. This was only half the amount given to the Hôtel de Bourgogne, but it was enough.

Actors have rarely been noted for charity to their rivals, and theatre politics are usually conducted on a level that would make Machiavelli blush with shame. The Hôtel de Bourgogne was no exception to this rule. Smarting from the loss of its unique privilege, it promptly pulled strings to raid the Marais and rob it of four of its best actors. Montdory ran in desperation to Richelieu, and secured the transfer of two of the Bourgogne company to his own. Throughout the years to come alliances shifted constantly. The Bourgogne was still the senior theatre, and could always use its prestige to charm away a dramatist, or lure promising players to its fold. Montdory retaliated with a brilliant season and a more heavily tragic repertoire, which was to bring about his greatest professional triumph and his greatest personal downfall. His theatrical sensation was the premiere of Corneille's *Le Cid*, which opened in January 1637 and took the town by storm. It had a plot of perennial attraction, lovers kept apart by force of circumstances. Montdory was superb in the title role of Don Rodrigue, with Mlle Villiers playing Chimène, and the Spanish setting provided an environment in which chivalry and heroics could be seen as part of real life, not merely as a stage convention. All Paris swarmed to see it. *Loges* and *parterre* were packed to bursting. Niches where pages and lackeys customarily stood had to be used for extra seating. The overflow crowd even spilled on to the stage, starting a theatrical habit which later years found it almost impossible to break: Voltaire, a century afterwards, was still trying to get the audience off the stage.

Out of this startling success arose new jealousies and quarrels. In a period when any new play had to appease a growing swarm of critics, *Le Cid* stands out as the major battleground over which the standards of contemporary playwriting were debated with a fierceness and rancour equal to the play's popular esteem. Dozens of pamphlets were circulated on the subject. Brother authors complained that Corneille was bringing the art into disrepute. He was accused of plagiarism, because he had stolen the play from Spanish sources; of immorality, because his heroine failed to comport herself like a gentlewoman; of various faults of tastes and style; and, more importantly, of failure to observe the canons of tragic composition that critics were reconstructing from classical sources. People on all social levels took sides, Richelieu was antagonised, and the whole affair was finally passed for judgement to the newly created Académie Française, whose limp response did nothing to increase their own prestige or diminish the author's. Le Cid has remained as one of the high marks of French dramatic achievement, constantly in the repertoire and providing innumerable budding actors with test pieces. The classical actor in the English theatre was once judged by his Richard III, and now tends to be judged by his Hamlet. His French counterpart is judged by his Don Rodrigue.

Montdory's personal tragedy was his disappearance from the stage in circumstances so melodramatic that, if presented in a play, they would be dismissed as improbable fiction. While playing the role of Herod in Tristan l'Hermite's Mariane, he underwent a fate like that attributed to Sophocles, so overtaxing his voice that he suffered a partial paralytic stroke. Deprived of the actor's chief instrument, he subsided into mute, irascible retirement, trying vainly to make a comeback and existing on a bare pension.

The incident shows how rapidly, in this as at all times, stage idols could be forgotten. It also tells us a good deal about the nature of French tragic acting.

The Marais, however, was firmly established. Passing under new management, it continued to draw the public with a series of new, though slightly more conservative, tragedies by Corneille. But the Hôtel de Bourgogne conducted another raid, and in January 1644 came what appeared to be a crushing blow when the theatre and its wardrobe were destroyed by fire. Friends of the company rushed to its aid. A new building rose rapidly from the ashes of the old, and the building contracts, which we still possess, allow us to assess the size of the reconstruction. The Marais was in fact able to turn disaster into profit by expanding its operation. The new auditorium was 125' long, bigger than the ordinary jeux de paume. There were two tiers of eighteen loges, surmounted by a paradis; a vast amphithéâtre; and, at last, some comfort for the actors in ten new dressing rooms behind the stage. The stage itself now had a raked platform and an upper level usable for 'scenes above' and the mechanical effects which were to be the later Marais's stock-in-trade. Now able to accommodate 1500 spectators, the restored Marais undoubtedly provoked the alterations to the Hôtel de Bourgogne a few years later.

Once again the Bourgogne raided, this time making off with the chief actor of the company and its new manager, Floridor. At this point the Marais seems to have accepted the inevitable and given up trying to rival the older theatre on its own ground. While tragedies continued to be given, they formed a diminishing part of the repertoire. More and more the Marais turned to pure spectacle and the 'machine play'. These will be discussed at greater length in a later chapter, but for the moment a selection of titles will serve to suggest the exotic material offered. The list includes *Circe* (men turned into beasts); *La Descente d'Orphée aux Enfers*; *Andromède et Persée* (an aerobatic hero, a beautiful captive princess, and a sea monster); *Les Amours de Jupiter et de Sémélé* (divine thunder and lightning) and *Les Amours de Vénus et Adonis*. Many of these were successful, luring the King to attend in person, but the fickle public was turning back to the Hôtel de Bourgogne and the period is substantially one of decline. The final, fatal blow was struck by the composer Jean Baptiste Lully, whom we shall meet again in connection with Molière. Lully, one of the shrewdest of contemporary entrepreneurs, was anxious to create his own monopoly in musical theatre. A royal patent granted him sole rights in staging opera in Paris, and he promptly used this to forbid any other theatre to use more than a token number of singers and instrumentalists in its productions. This made musical spectaculars impossible, and the Marais limped to a sad close, finally merging with Molière's company after the latter's death to form the *troupe du Roi à l'Hôtel de Guénégaud*. The world of the theatre is seldom a just one, but the Marais had suffered more than its share of unfairness. It must have been some consolation that a few years later the Hôtel de Bourgogne was also forced to close its doors and merge with the combined company.

We have seen some of the principal stages, and must now examine what went on within them. In scene design, as in everything else, this was a period of transition. Just as the organisation of the theatre changed from amateur to professional, and the subject matter of plays from sacred to secular, so the nature of stage settings could not avoid being influenced by the shift from outdoors to indoors, from large open spaces to small confined ones. The medieval pageant play was all-embracing in its setting, just as it was cosmic in its argument. Dispersed round the huge playing-space, the audience enjoyed what we might call a God's-eye view of the action. All the locations required were spread out before them at once, with Heaven on one side and Hell on the other, and an action which covered centuries of historical time, and thousands of miles of space, was seen in a single panoramic view. For example, in the Rouen *Mystery of the Incarnation* and *Nativity of our Saviour and Redeemer Jesus Christ* we have a succession of short scenes encompassing the 'places of the Prophets'; the mansion of the Sibyl, the Emperor's palace, and various other places in Rome; Limbo; Rome again; Paradise; Hell;

the road to Rome; various places in Rome itself; Jerusalem; Bethlehem; Paradise; Nazareth – and so the list goes on. The actors moved from one location to another as required, and a journey from Rome to Jerusalem could be accomplished in a matter of seconds. This does not represent, as some people once believed, any kind of medieval naïveté about the physical world. Such a view is itself naïve. Rather, the medieval practice communicates the sense that all things are as one in the sight of the Creator, and that in the divine scheme such earthly considerations as time or place have little meaning. The whole universe is seen as one, and past and present exist contemporaneously. In keeping with this concept, settings are emblematic rather than realistic; or rather, they are little islands of spatial and temporal realism floating in a void. The wheeled platforms which are trundled into the arena may suggest the location and give it a temporary anchor in our space and time, but do not rigidly define or confine it. All is open and flexible.

The immediate effect of moving indoors, into a more restricted viewing space, was that the scope of such a scenic picture was no longer possible. In some special cases, the older concept of dispersed staging could continue without unease. This was true, for instance, of the court ballets, allegorical entertainments of great splendour and complexity, which unfolded in halls scarcely smaller than the outdoor arenas. Here, therefore, the medieval concept of separate, self-contained scenic 'mansions' was able to perpetuate itself; some particular examples will be discussed in a later chapter. But with the commercial theatre the case was different, and the transition painful. Our evidence comes mainly from the *Mémoire* of Laurent Mahelot, with a series of designs, either by Mahelot himself or a collaborator, for the Hôtel de Bourgogne up to 1635. These designs, though often beautiful and always skilful, reflect the incongruity of trying to compress the old sense of panoramic action within the limits of a small picture-frame stage. The anomalies are more patent. Though no longer present in kind, the medieval mansions are replaced in essence by separate scenic units – wings, groundrows, back-drops – each indicating a separate locale, but with only a few feet of space between them. What was plausible in terms of the old conventions has become absurd in terms of the new. It is this incongruity that prompts Corneille's objection, already quoted, to the practice of compressing Rome, Paris and Constantinople within the same dramatic action.

New drama forms, then, demand a new stage space. It is not merely a question of enclosing the scene with roof and walls. The issue is deeper than that, and involves the whole question of what drama should be, and how the spectator should relate to it. We have noticed how the characteristic structure of French theatres was influenced by their temporary predecessors. We might also notice how the interior dispositions of these theatres were influenced by the kind of audience they now housed. Division into *loges* and *parterre*, as distinct from the great amorphous crowd-mass that watched the mystery plays, bespeaks an aristocratic-bourgeois society conscious of its own social differentiations; the box represents the unit of the family from which this society is constructed. With enlargements and elaborations, the *loge* concept dominated European theatre design for the next three hundred years.

For the God's-eye view of the medieval spectator his seventeenth-century counterpart substituted a man's-eye view. His world, both physically and metaphysically, had shrunk. Physically, as the dimensions of theatres show, his viewpoint could be very limited indeed. Instead of looking at the world spread out before him, he looked through a peephole at a segment of this world. Unless he were seated dead centre, his view could be even worse hampered; significantly, the Hôtel de Bourgone reserved as its house seats – those given to complimentary ticket-holders – a few places tucked away in the *amphithéâtre* or the corners of the balcony tiers. These obviously commanded the worst view in the house. At court performances the rank and file fared even worse, for the whole production was frankly accommodated to one man's view – the one man in this case being the King, who sat full centre on a dais, in what would be the *parterre* of a commercial theatre. To him the actors played; to his sightlines the false perspective of the setting would conform, so that only the King would have a perfect and undistorted view. There is a certain symbolic importance in this.

Just as the spectator's field of vision had narrowed, so did the world of the play. It dealt now with secular, not sacred, material and with actions more human than divine, framed in a human context and enforcing greater concentration on human limitations of time and place. The extent to which French dramatists voluntarily chose to submit to such strict limitations will be discussed in a later chapter. Aesthetically, and in terms of stage dynamics, the change is similar to what occurred in the English theatre when the open, fluid and scenically unrestricted Elizabethan stage gave way to the pictorialised representations of the Restoration and later. In France, the stage picture now became more localised and more realistic, aided by the advances in illusionistic false perspective inspired by Italian designers and increasingly available for study. The theatre remained, however, highly selective in the pictures it chose to present to its audiences; though the subject-matter of drama was secular, it was rarely mundane, and spectators grew accustomed, at least in tragedy, to a succession of classically-inspired palaces in which characters of high stature sought to resolve their problems. Even in comedy, upper-class houses or places of smart social resort provided the bulk of the settings. French drama, like its audience, was snobbishly inclined. On stage the actors, instead of being able to select and dictate their own environment by moving from one locale to another, were now confined within the environment which had been imposed upon them. More and more, the shape of the scenic room came to dictate the shape of the play.

We have confined ourselves so far to formal theatres and formally organised companies. There were others, at both extremes of the social scale. The clowns and quack doctors continued to perform in the streets and market-places. In the *faubourgs* ringing the city walls, annual fairs housed both theatres and puppet shows. All of these in various ways gave sustenance to the theatre proper. In the mansions of the great, and particularly at Versailles, which became the cultural showplace of the new regime, the King himself wore costume, and companies performed by light of torch and moon in pavilions erected for the occasion. But it is with the theatres proper that we must still concern ourselves. We shall look now at the circumstances in which the journeyman actor lived and performed, and the sort of career he could expect now that a professional theatre was available to him.

3 The Company at Work

As the market for plays increased, the companies multiplied. So far we have been dealing only with some of the fortunate few who were able to locate themselves in Paris. But these were only a fraction of the whole. It has been shown that, from the closing years of the sixteenth century to the opening decade of the eighteenth, there were over two hundred companies working in France, and over a thousand actors. Many of these never saw Paris. They were contented with the provincial circuits and with towns which gradually established themselves as secondary theatre centres, such as Rouen, Lyons and, when it eventually became a French possession, Lille. The existence of these companies has been painstakingly catalogued from local archives, but in most cases we know little more than the name of the company and the towns where it played. We have the statistics, but lack the human interest which would bring those statistics to life.

There is, however, one company about which we know a good deal. Though it has so far been mentioned only in passing, it was one of the most famous of them all: the company headed by the man who called himself Molière, which started from the humblest beginnings, survived all the hazards of life on tour, finally established itself in Paris and challenged and eventually absorbed the troupes of the Marais and the Bourgogne. Through these people we gain our clearest insight into the workaday lives of French actors – their rewards and tribulations, their successes and failures, their rare moments of glory and their more frequent humiliations. We can feel what it was like to work in a period of such ambivalence, when the actor could be lauded as an artist but slighted as a human being. To say that we know a good deal about Molière and his colleagues, however, is not to say that we know all. In some aspects we know them so well that they become almost palpable, reaching out of history across the void of years to touch us. In others they remain enigmas, and we are as puzzled by them as by an old dear friend who has portions of his life that he will not let us share.

This is particularly true of Molière himself, a man about whom we should like to know a great deal more than we do. If Molière was the Shakespeare of France in the sense that his plays both summed up an age and established a dramatic pattern that would endure for centuries after, he is no less like Shakespeare in the conundrums he has bequeathed to his biographers. In their enigmas, the two men are remarkably similar. In both cases there are important gaps in the records, obscuring crucial portions of the author's personal life and artistic development. The very existence of these gaps tells us something about contemporary attitudes towards theatre practitioners, and the amount of remarkably silly scholarship which came into existence on both sides of the Channel shows what happened when these early attitudes had to be changed. In each case we see, first, a lack of attention towards an author who, in his time, could be stigmatised as a mere player, and dismissed as one hack writer among many; and then, when time has worked its familiar changes and hindsight has revealed the subject to be a literary figure of substance, we find this neglect replaced by frenetic and over-imaginative efforts to reconstruct material irremediably lost. For example, we have nothing in Shakespeare's own hand beyond a few signatures, and for Molière little more. We can reconstruct some parts of Shakespeare's early life and education; we can do the same for Molière's first years in the theatre in almost painful detail. But for both men the vital period, when the tiro transformed himself into the master, has been largely lost to us. We can study the retirement of the one and the miserable death of the other, but too much of what goes before remains shadowy.

Consequently both dramatists have come down to us as partial mysteries, presenting serious critics with dilemmas and exciting the lunatic fringe of scholarship to frenzies of invention. In Shakespeare's case, it has been argued that a common player with a barely adequate education could never have composed the glowing, informed masterpieces attributed to him. Thus some other author must be found, who used Shakespeare as a pen-name – Francis Bacon, Christopher Marlowe, the Earls of Oxford and Southampton, Queen Elizabeth, take your choice. So with Molière. Could a strolling player, a tradesman's son, have written those urbane, luminous comedies? Never! It must have been Corneille himself, writing under a pseudonym but revealing his identity to the initiated, like Bacon, through anagrams: the names Molière and Corneille, if you omit the right letters, are anagrams of each other. Or else it was Louis XIV himself '*sous le masque de Molière*'. (Curious that the mask, so crucial to the staging and psychology of Molière's plays, should have been enfolded by the legends.) Even the recorded facts of

Molière's life have been called into question and turned into mysteries. He did not die, it is alleged, when he was reported to have died. Instead he was arrested, sent to the Bastille and became . . . the Man in the Iron Mask.

But, setting this nonsense aside, what do we know? Less than we should like, but enough. We learn of the son of a respectable bourgeois household, trained, expected and for a time even willing to follow his father's trade as an upholsterer, with a minor court appointment and an entrée into the lower echelons of the palace administration. There is no hint of the performing arts in his background, save for a line of distant relatives who worked as court musicians. Then came the change that sparked his life. In June 1643 we find the young Jean Baptiste Poquelin, as he still was – he had yet to take his stage name – signing a contract for the formation of a theatre company. Among the co-signatories are members of the Béjart family with which his life was thereafter to be inextricably linked; and particularly Madeleine Béjart, possibly a remote connection who was to become his mistress and perhaps his mother-in-law but who remained his actress all her life. A later satirical pamphlet, in play form puts into Molière's mouth a soliloquy describing his supposed theatrical beginnings:

> But being unemployed, I did debate
> Where best my talents could advance the State,
> And saw that only on the stage I'd find
> An outlet worthy of my brilliant mind . . .
> I looked for actors blessed with gifts like mine
> To lend distinction to this grand design,
> But everyone of merit turned me down!
> So, since I could not hire the best in town,
> I settled for the dregs, of whom the prize
> Limped, stuttered, or had lost one of his eyes.
> For women . . . I approached the fairest ever
> But blonde and brunette both said bluntly 'Never!'
> Back to the redhead. Though she smelt a bit,
> With scent and powder I put up with it.

The lady thus ungallantly described is Madeleine; the powder may have been for her hair rather than a deodorant, as the Parisian audience seems to have disliked redheads, and she may have been compelled to tone it down. Grimarest, Molière's first serious biographer, gives a more sympathetic view of their association, suggesting that 'it was common enough at that time for people to give amateur performances to entertain their friends. Some of the Paris *bourgeoisie* formed such a group, with Molière as one of the members, and put on a number of performances for their own amusement.' It may indeed have been this kind of diversion that inspired Molière to change careers. It may have been the direct urging of the Béjarts. This is one of the things that we can never really know.

But the contract remains, and it shows one of the most unlikely groups of people ever to have committed themselves to a professional theatre venture. A few already had limited professional experience. Madeleine may have been one of them. We know at least that she had been stage-struck from an early age. Like any modern teenage fan, she had written adoring verses to one of the popular dramatists, Rotrou. She was distantly related to another, Tristan l'Hermite. Living near the Marais, she may have walked on in the 1636 production of *Mariamne*, when the great Montdory played Herod. Others were mere novices, like Denis Beys, a bookseller (though his brother, Charles, was a playwright), Nicolas Bonnenfant, a law clerk, or Molière himself, who at twenty-one had no theatrical background at all apart from what he might have picked up by talking to the players in Les Halles. Probably his main contribution was to underwrite the venture. Despite his theatrical virginity he appears in the contract as one of four actors given as their right a choice of roles. It reads suspiciously like a quid pro quo.

But good will had to be translated into action. Other documents show the steps taken to realise the grand design. These were the same practical problems that attended every company. A *jeu de paume* was hired, optimistically, on a three-year lease. *Loges* and other seats were constructed, and a stage built. The *porte cochère* was paved for the carriage trade which it was hoped would come. Plays were selected. But this was a new and untried group in an unfashionable location, and successful playwrights were obviously unwilling to trust it, even though it had been christened with the proud name Illustre Théâtre. One playwright who did show faith was Jean Magnon, a theatrical fledgling like Molière himself and from the same sort of background, a family in trade at Lyons and a Jesuitical education. He gave the company his first play, *Artaxerxes*, and prospered better than the Illustre Théâtre did, for we later find him writing for the Hôtel de Bourgogne. Tristan l'Hermite was another; as we have seen, Madeleine may have been able to appeal to him through various connections. In 1636 *Mariane* had elevated him to stunning success, but since then he had written little, and his name was fading from the public mind. He may have welcomed a company, any company, that was prepared to give his plays a hearing. The Illustre Théâtre played with some success his *The Death of Seneca*. It was based on an account in Tacitus of a plot against the Emperor Nero in which Seneca was unwillingly involved; the play ended with Seneca's forced suicide. Tristan's play is still extant, and seems a dull thing to us now. It drags through endless Senecan debates on whether to join the conspiracy or not; and for Molière's company it must have posed some casting problems, having nine male roles to be apportioned among only six actors. Madeleine at least did well as Epicharis, a slave girl compelled to submit to Nero's torture, and Molière, far too young for Seneca, may have played the Emperor himself.

One critic has called these years the 'growth period' of the French theatre. Molière's company declined. Too many things were against it: inexperience, competition from the senior houses, a bad location on the Left, unfashionable, Bank and a lacklustre repertoire. Surviving documents show the onset of hardship. Bills came in, and remained unpaid. Moving to the Right Bank the company sought a more attractive home; but it was still unfashionable, still too far off centre. Ominously, new contracts substituted 'for as long as the theatre shall continue' for the old 'three years'. Legal action was threatened. Finally the Illustre Théâtre, after a less than illustrious season, closed its doors, leaving Molière with a pile of debts, some hard-won experience, his stage name and an appetite for more.

The story of the next twelve years suggests what it must have meant to belong to a company touring in the provinces. It is not a complete picture, for records of actual performances are few and far between. Our information comes mainly from more prosaic documents, ferreted out by French scholars with their usual meticulous care from local archives. We have records of births and marriages, attesting to the presence of the company at a given place; we have notes of loans signed for and witnessed. We have occasional indications of hard times, when the company was forced to other, more dubious means of support. What this period did for Molière as a writer we can only guess; but we can guess intelligently. He must have profited from other companies he met, particularly the Italians touring in the South of France. He must have learnt speed and deftness of composition, discovering how to fabricate new plays out of familiar materials, how to appeal to local audiences. One of the most famous legends of this time tells of Molière's trunk, packed with manuscripts and lost in the rush between one town and another. The contents of that fabulous trunk have often been 'rediscovered', and almost as often they have turned out to be palpable forgeries. As well as learning the writer's trade, Molière must have made firm his actor's craft and acquired assurance, for we find him emerging as head of the troupe that he had joined as a journeyman player. Imagination can colour his voyages. We can sense the pressures of the constant move from place to place, the strain on a company without a permanent home; the rattling arrival by coach or cart, the hiring of a theatre – perhaps a real playhouse, if the town, like Lyons, had one, or a converted *jeu de paume* or barn; the posted bills, the trumpeted announcements; the dressing amid cramped surroundings in the canvas breastplates and monstrously plumed helmets of tragedy, or last year's fashions for comedy; the performance of a rustic farce quickly written and hastily but adequately rehearsed by actors who knew one another's strengths and mannerisms inside out.

Our documents add one important dimension: the sense of the company as a family. In their visible deportment and internal organisation, actors have commonly tended to model themselves on the world around them; it is a useful form of protective colouration, particularly in societies where the theatre is suspect. Thus we see the Elizabethan actors forming themselves along the lines of the respectable craft guilds; the touring companies of the nineteenth century in America assuming a respectable, even devout aspect to allow them to operate with tolerance in the Bible belt; the eminence of the paternalistic actor manager in the family-centred society of Victorian England. In Molière's time actors had two models. Living in a society which had the king as its heart and centre, and was dominated by a small, powerful and exclusive aristocracy, they sought reflected glory by modelling themselves on the nobility. They adopted stage names which were flowery and magniloquent. They assumed the aristocratic cachet *de*, and sometimes even an actual title. Mlle du Parc, who had begun her career as a child rope dancer and later turned *comédienne*, was professionally known as the Marquise.

In their internal organisation, however, the actors' model was the French bourgeois family, which has been defined as one of the tightest and most protective social units that the world has ever produced. The company formed a collection of individuals with well-defined relationships, united for mutual assurance and financial security, with a group sense that transcended personal idiosyncracies. France, perhaps more than any country in the world, has developed a feeling of the personality of the institution, over and above the personalities of its individual members; and nowhere is this more clearly in evidence than in the

French theatre. In the company we are now considering, Molière emerges as the father-figure, the controller, and for a long time the *orateur*, or public spokesman, for the troupe. If there is a mother-figure, it is Madeleine. The other actors and actresses, the 'children', arranged themselves in various combinations. Driven in upon themselves by social prejudice, they tended to marry within the profession and to bring up their children to follow in their footsteps. They stood as godparents to the children of their colleagues. In Molière's last play, *Le Malade Imaginaire* (*The Imaginary Invalid*) the actor Beauval plays one of the leading roles, his wife plays the scheming servant, and their child, *la petite Beauval*, plays the main character's little daughter. Young players might expect to grow to maturity within the protection of the company, as Molière's young wife did; and Michel Baron, the most brilliant young actor of his time, was by all accounts virtually an adopted son.

In most of their actions the members of the company manifested a strong group loyalty. Sometimes, as in any family, there could be squabbles; sometimes individuals would grow wilful and desert. Thus, in Paris, the Marais on several occasions lost actors to the Bourgogne, not always by compulsion; thus, also, Molière lost a playwright, Racine, to the Bourgogne, and with him the Marquise du Parc who had become Racine's mistress. But on the whole the actors stayed, if not to their deaths, at least to a pensioned retirement to which their colleagues contributed. There can be no greater tribute to this group cohesiveness than the willingness and ability of Molière's company to continue to function, with barely a missed performance, after the death of the man who had been their guide and inspiration for so many years.

Well-conducted families keep their financial affairs in order. Molière's company, like others, worked on the share system, whereby the profits, greater or less, were divided among the actors on an equal basis. Molière was entitled to an additional share as author, which was no more than just. It was in this period that dramatic authors first began seriously to claim their rights. Up to this time they had largely been considered as hacks, writing on demand and selling their plays like so much merchandise, with no further rights or interest in their work once it had been purchased by the company. But the new French playwrights benefited from increased critical attention, found themselves regarded as figures of literary stature, and advanced rapidly towards a level of esteem that their English counterparts had only achieved by a long and arduous process. Appropriate financial reward followed, with larger fees demanded and paid and the first, tentative beginnings of a system of author's royalties.

For the families within the larger family, actors with working wives received a second share. Such an arrangement was made for Molière in 1661, in provision for his marriage the year following to a girl who was already acting with the company. A contemporary play gives a sidelight on the actors' working routine by showing them splitting up the daily take. This is Corneille's *L'Illusion Comique*, a tragicomedy full of deaths and misunderstandings which are revealed at the end to have been only part of a play: 'At this point', says the stage direction, 'the curtain is raised and all the actors appear with their doorkeeper, counting out the money on a table, with everyone taking his due share.' A speech follows hailing the glories of the theatre and the possibilities that it offers for worldly success:

> The theatre today – do not despise it –
> Has grown so great that all men idolize it.
> The art your generation did reject
> Is courted now by wit and intellect.
> In town, all go there; out of town, all try.
> It is the favourite sport of royalty,
> Adored by lord and common man alike,
> Their cherished pastime, and their chief delight. . . .
> And if you measure people by their wealth
> The stage gives ample means to enrich yourself.
> By choosing this vocation to pursue
> Your son will do much better than with you!

This may have been true for Corneille, who had a reputation for being careful of his financial interests. It was true for a few leading actors who, from public esteem or private patronage, reaped handsome rewards. But to the rank and file of the profession, Corneille's rosy picture must have been simply another agreeable stage fiction.

Company responsibility did not end with financial matters. In the first contract of the Illustre Théâtre, we see artistic control vested in the group as a whole. This appears to have been common practice. It became customary, when dealing with outside authors, for a member of the troupe to act as the playwright's representative and present a new work for approval. It was read and discussed, and, if the play was accepted, parts were distributed according to established rights and privileges. In most cases casting was automatic, since actors tended to specialise in certain types of roles. As illustration of this we may look at another play, *Le Véritable Saint Genest* (*The True Saint Genesius*) written by

Jean Rotrou in 1645. It is the story of the Roman mime who, while parodying Christian rites to amuse his pagan audience, was converted in mid-performance, suffered death rather than renounce his new faith, and became the patron saint of actors. It is thus largely a play about actors and how they work; and though it is set in fourth-century Rome, the local colour and theatrical detail are unmistakeably those of seventeenth-century France. When Genesius' troupe is being interrogated by the imperial officer, we have the following dialogue:

PLANCIEN	What roles have you played?
MARCELLE	Women, as you've seen.
	Except that, if the play demands, I can
	Change costume, and impersonate a man.
PLANCIEN	And you?
OCTAVE	One day the slave, the next the king.
PLANCIEN	You?
SERGESTE	Swaggering heroes, bold and blustering.
PLANCIEN	And you, old man?
LENTULE	Quack doctors, learned fools,
	Sometimes the hero's friend, or villains' roles.
PLANCIEN	And you?
ALBIN	The extras.

In Molière's company as it ultimately established itself casting tended to follow similar 'lines of business'. La Grange, a later addition to the troupe, was normally given the 'straight' lover's roles. Molière continued to play, to the end of his days, the athletic, acrobatic parts in which he had first made his name. There must have been some competition for the *ingénue* roles. They were divided among Molière's young wife Armande, the Marquise du Parc and Mlle de la Thorillière. One of the saddest features of the cast-lists is that they show Madeleine growing old. Although she may occasionally capture a stunning character part like the matchmaker Frosine in *L'Avare* (*The Miser*) she appears more and more as the *suivante*, supporting the leading lady. Perhaps the cruellest note of all is that in 1664, when the company performed a ballet at Versailles, Madeleine appeared on a bear, representing winter.

Like so many features of the seventeenth century theatre, this concept of company rule has continued to dominate later practice. The Comédie Française has always clung to the family concept, distinguishing between *pensionnaires* and *sociétaires*, temporary and permanent, members. Casting was done for years on hierarchical principles, with the leading roles going by right to the senior members, often to the detriment of the performance; audiences might sometimes have to watch a Cyrano de Bergerac who was too old to duel. The company still meets formally to discuss new plays. Jean-Louis Barrault has left a vivid account of his attempts to secure his colleagues' acceptance of Claudel. But in spite of the occasional, inevitable eccentricities of such a system, its strength persists. New members, carefully selected are welcomed with appropriate social ceremonies. Actors of the Comédie proudly proclaim their affiliation when they work outside, and though they may sever legal ties with the family they never really leave it. Molière would feel at home in the theatre that has come to be known as the *maison de Molière*.

But we have anticipated, for we left Molière still in the provinces. His company, with a new confidence in its abilities, returned to Paris in 1658. Its members had learnt the hard way, like other companies before them, that in the dog-eat-dog world of the theatre security was impossible without patronage. Here again the French pattern resembles the English of a century before. Just as the London-based companies had sought sponsorship from the Earl of Leicester, the Lord Admiral, or members of the royal family, so French companies had from the beginning sheltered under the power of great names, ranging from the Prince of Orange to Richelieu himself. This gave some status to a stigmatised profession; it held some promise of financial subsidy; and, at the least, it offered protection from the sporadic harassment of civil and ecclesiastical authorities. In the provinces Molière had enjoyed the patronage of the Prince de Conti, who was later, in an access of misguided religious zeal, to change sides and write a polemic directed mainly against the man whose talent he had done much to foster. The fickleness of princes was a factor to be reckoned with, and Louis XIV himself was to prove hardly less wayward. By 1658, however, Molière had found no less impressive a sponsor than the King's brother, Monsieur, and it was under his auspices that the company played before royalty in the Salle des Gardes (now the Salle des Cariatides) in the Louvre.

That October day has become famous in theatre history. Molière offered two plays. The first was *Nicomède* (*Nicomedes*), a tragedy by Corneille. At first sight, this seems a curious choice. It was already some eight years old, and had been performed, probably better, by the Hôtel de Bourgogne, the established masters of tragedy in the capital. And yet it was appropriate for the circumstances. *Nicomède* is drawn from the history of the Roman Republic, immediately after the final defeat of Hannibal in the Punic Wars. Its subject is the jostling for power among

the potentates of Asia Minor and the attempts of Rome to assert her
own influence through favoured candidates. What had all this to do
with Louis XIV? A good deal. A play which showed a domineering
Queen Mother and a Machiavellian foreign politician; which showed a
young, handsome, brave and generous prince coming into his own;
which began with plots by the powerful against the throne, and ended
in an aura of reconciliation and forgiveness, with even his former
enemies acknowledging the new monarch's greatness: such a work had
obvious appeal for a young king who had emerged from one of the most
troubled periods of French internal politics and who was to insist on the
supreme authority of the monarch. *Nicomède*, in fact, strikes a note
which continues to reverberate through the plays of the period: flattery
of the ruler, and attention drawn to Louis XIV as the all-good, the
great dispenser, saviour and provider. Nor was such praise necessarily
insincere.

The second offering was *Le Docteur Amourex* (*The Doctor in Love*),
one of Molière's own rustic farces. If *Nicomède* had a tepid reception,
the comedy was wildly successful. We may guess that its appeal lay in
its freshness and vitality, exciting to an audience whose palate had been
jaded by a stream of more sophisticated offerings. It gave Molière a
footing in Paris, a theatre, and the assurance of royal support. He now
felt able to compete on equal terms with the Marais and the Bourgogne.

But establishment in Paris did not bring relief. It merely replaced one
kind of worry by another. First there was the daily drudgery of commercial theatre management. Although he had been given a playhouse,
the Salle du Petit Bourbon, Molière was never totally secure. At first he
had to share with a rival company of Italian players and work on the
jours extraordinaires; the *jours ordinaires*, on which plays were normally
given, were Tuesday, Friday and Sunday. Next, the theatre was demo-
lished while the company was still in occupancy; it was part of the
rebuilding programme that no one had bothered to inform Molière
about. After a brief, homeless period he moved into the theatre Richelieu
had built for his own Palais Cardinal, bequeathed to the King as the
Palais Royal. This remained Molière's permanent home until his death.
But the theatre had to be filled with plays, either his own or others'. The
season began after Easter and ran for the best part of the year, devouring
material. Molière's season for 1660–1 included his own *Le Cocu Imaginaire* (*The Imaginary Cuckold*), *Les Précieuses Ridicules* (*The Affected
Young Ladies*), *Le Dépit Amoureux* (*The Lovers' Quarrel*) and
L'Etourdi (*The Blunderer*) together with revivals of Corneille's *Nicomède*, *Rodogune* and *Heraclius*, Rotrou's *Venceslas* and Gilbert's *Les*

Amours de Diane et Endymion. But putting together a season was never easy, since rival companies fought for competent dramatists. It would not be long before Molière, who had first cultivated Racine, was to lose him to the Bourgogne.

We have ample evidence for the company's financial administration in two documents. One is the Register of Charles Varlet de la Grange, who joined the troupe in 1659 and worked as bookkeeper in addition to his acting roles. This is a personal as well as a financial record; it lists the births, deaths and marriages among the personnel together with the receipts from Molière's productions. These fluctuated to an enormous degree. *Tartuffe*, a controversial play from the beginning, broke all box office records when it was finally allowed on the public stage and continued to be an assured money-maker for a long time. *Psyche*, a spectacular ballet-drama originally commissioned for a royal command performance, was another instant success when it was transferred to the commercial theatre. But these were balanced by works of less appeal, and a comparison of La Grange's figures with Molière's output shows the constant necessity on the playwright to consider the popular taste, and redeem the comparative failure of a more serious work by a rapid return to broad farce. For the expenses always had to be met. A breakdown of the payroll at the end of the 1659–60 season shows the normal pattern. It includes payments to four box-openers (ancestors of today's usherettes), two box-office personnel, the scene-painter, the theatre janitor and violinists (presumably for the regular pre-show and interval music). Candles for lighting were a major expense. So were posters; our sole surviving example from this period happens to be one advertising Molière's company as the *Troupe de Monsieur*. There is an entry for 'food and drink', presumably to feed the company when they could not leave the theatre. Extraordinary productions involved extraordinary expenses. *Psyché*, smash hit though it was, necessitated the hiring of large numbers of extra personnel: adult and child dancers, additional musicians, extras for the crowd scenes, operators for the complex and spectacular stage machinery and builders for the new constructions. Every production was a gamble.

We have further information from another account-book, this time kept by the actor Hubert. As well as creating several notable comic roles – he was the original Madame Jourdain in *Le Bourgeois Gentilhomme*, conceived as a 'pantomime dame' part – Hubert was involved with the operation of the box-office, and has left detailed records of the season 1672–3. Analysis shows the extent to which the monthly takings at the Palais Royal could vary. November, the height of the theatrical season, brought a peak audience of 7449. In March, just before the annual recess, this had dropped to 3790. Gloomy statistics show that the company could rarely count on playing to a full house.

But as well as this regular activity, a company enjoying royal patronage had to stand ready to respond to royal whims and prepare special entertainments on command, often at ludicrously short notice. In *L'Impromptu de Versailles*, written for such an occasion, Molière makes capital out of this too familiar problem by writing a play about not having time to write a play. He shows his actors as themselves, desperately trying to cobble something together, and in the process makes some wry comments on the exigencies of court favour:

> God knows, Mademoiselle, kings like instant obedience above all things else. Once you start putting obstacles in their way, they aren't happy in the least. When there's something they want, they want it now. As soon as you ask for a postponement, you take away all their pleasure in the show. The shorter the preparation, the better they like it. In thinking over what they ask of us, we ought never to consider ourselves. We exist only for their pleasure. When they commission something from us, its our business to make a quick profit from their passing fancy. Better do what they ask and do it fast, than not do it fast enough.

Thus the life of the company in Paris was punctuated by visits to the great chateaux or to Versailles itself, the mecca of high society. Rotrou, in *Saint Genest*, gives a snatch of the kind of conversation that must often have gone on between actor-managers and their overworked staff, plagued by royal importunities, the necessity of mounting as impressive a show as possible, and sheer lack of time.

GENEST   It's good enough, but still, with small expense
You could improve on its magnificence.
Let in more daylight. Take away the gloom.
Add stature to the trimmings of the room –
Marble facade and jasper colonnade,
Pillars with drums and capitals arrayed . . .
And on the backdrop where you paint your skies
Make them appear more natural to the eyes.
They look somewhat funereal to me!

SCENE PAINTER   It's time we lack, and not the energy!
Moreover, if you would not stand so near

The contrast and relief would show more clear.
Too close a view destroys the false perspective,
Blurs highlights, and makes colours less effective.
Just as in nature, so in our department;
Closeness offends, and distance lends enchantment!

Actors, like their managers, had to be versatile and adaptable to changes of circumstance; to carry a large repertoire in their heads; and to be adept in dance and song. When we ask how the actor approached his role, and in what terms he presented himself to his audience, we find a variety of answers, depending on the individual, the company he worked for, and the nature of his dramatic medium. As in any age, some were clearly 'personality' actors, depending on their mannerisms or physical attractions to hold an audience. Leading ladies relied heavily on their personal beauty. In *Le Bourgeois Gentilhomme* Molière has left us a charming picture of his wife Armande, who created the role of Lucile. The description of the character is clearly that of the actress. She is dainty, petite, with lustrous eyes, a seductive mouth and a carefree manner – spoiled, but charming. It is a description that belies the heavy, rather forbidding portraits of Armande that have survived. The Marquise du Parc must have been a similar stage charmer. She was known as *la dehanchée*, from the way she swayed her hips, and had three playwrights fall in love with her. First was the ageing Corneille, who saw her when the company played at Rouen and wrote her a sad December-May poem:

Marquise, remember; if my brow
Betrays the ravages of time,
When you are as old as I am now
Your state will be the same as mine.
That wastrel Time, who ever seeks
To banish loveliness and grace
Will pluck the roses from your cheeks
As he has furrowed this my face.
The same revolving sun and stars
Count off the days for you and me.
As you appear now, once I was,
And as I am, you too shall be.

Her next lover, according to gossip, was Molière himself, and last came Racine, for whom she left Molière to go to the Bourgogne. Rotrou, in

Saint Genest, gives us a view of such a star actress mobbed by admirers at a court performance:

MARCELLE   Good gods! How can an artist work here, pray?
                So many tiresome bores I've met today,
                So many broken hearts, to hear them tell,
                So many admirers captured by my spell! . . .
                If true, I'd have good reason for conceit.
                In my dressing room, they fought to kiss my feet,
                Till I could stand their flattery no more,
                Left them inside, came out, and shut the door!
                My adoring public! Worse than death I hate them,
                Their spite! Their gossip! And yet we create them;
                The very character of our profession
                Compels us to endure them with discretion.

You may pretend to hate them, comments her leading man wryly, but you love them really; and you spend all your time with them when you should be rehearsing.

An actor's personality was, of course, an exploitable commodity, and playwrights of this period had the great advantage of writing for a known company, rather than, as normally in the modern theatre, a group assembled for one production only. Molière was particularly skilful at adapting his performers' physical characteristics to the roles he wrote for them: Louis Béjart's limp, for example, and his own shortness of breath. But there were still certain basic requirements for an actor, fundamental skills on which he could build his performance; and for tragedy at least the most important of these, far more important than in the modern theatre, was a trained voice.

From the beginning French classical tragedy had been cast in a rhetorical mould. This was largely due to the Greek and Roman influences which weighed so heavily upon the art, and particularly to the Latin tragedies of Seneca, which – though probably never intended for stage performance – preferred reported to direct action, and used the plot as a framework on which to hang enormous expository or admonitory speeches, replete with the ornate devices of formal rhetoric. French authors could find similar models in their own society. Jodelle's *Cléopâtre Captive,* the first 'classical' tragedy, has been compared to a dirge, or a set of formal eulogies, in which the disaster is known from the beginning and the characters have nothing left to do but comment on their fate. As the new drama developed, the rhetorical influence continued to predominate. Even more than its Greek and Roman examplars, French tragedy preferred talk to action: patterned, beautiful, exciting talk, but still talk. It was incumbent upon the actor to develop a vocal instrument capable of communicating both the forcefulness of such rhetoric and its delicate nuances.

Tragic acting, then, was primarily a vocal, almost an operatic, performance, demanding great lung power and rigid breath control. We have seen the disaster suffered by Montdory at the Marais, when he overstrained his voice and ruined his career. Montfleury at the Bourgogne suffered a similar, though less permanent disability. These stories testify to the amount of sheer physical exertion that the actor was expected to bring to his part. But most of this was in the voice; stage movement and physical business were restricted, partly by a rigid concept of stage decorum and partly by the confines in which the player was forced to act. We have already noted the limited dimensions of the commercial theatres; added to this was the frequent hazard of audiences seated on the stage. Contemporary illustrations show that for special performances or overflow crowds tiers of benches could be set up round the acting area, so crowding the action that the audience was sometimes uncertain whether a new arrival was a late member of the public or a character making an entrance in the play. These considerations induced and supported a style of acting that was largely static and declamatory; a style, by our standards, totally artificial and divorced from the speech and gestures of everyday life. The actor acquired a mode of behaviour formulated by art rather than by nature, self-consistent in its context but as 'unreal' as the painted settings within which it was framed. Where a modern actor seeks psychological identification with his role, his seventeenth-century counterpart was more concerned with the externals, with moves and speech-patterns composed by rule, prescribed by tradition and learned by rote.

Something of this attitude still clings to the contemporary French theatre. The Paris Conservatoire, the breeding ground for the Comédie Française, still teaches its students to work with the maximum of voice and the minimum of gesture. Audiences who attend the final public *examens* have come to regard the great speeches virtually as operatic arias, and will compare the merits of the new candidates with the way in which Louis Jouvet or Gerard Philippe recited the same roles in the past, just as opera devotees compare different singers in Mozart. And one may still find French actors of the old school who cling firmly to the belief that their principal function is to stand still and declaim the lines.

Given such conditions, to what extent was an actor mentally and emotionally involved with his role? The question of how much should be technique, and how much nature, is one that every actor has to ask, and answer to his own satisfaction; and it was first formulated systematically by French critics of the eighteenth century on the basis of their own traditional theatre practice. They still came down heavily, for the most part, in favour of technique, and it seems clear that this is how most actors worked in Molière's time and continued to work for long afterwards. Diderot, in *Le Paradoxe sur le Comédien* (*The Paradox of Acting*) gives a delightful parody of an actor and an actress who are playing a highly emotional scene but are so uninvolved in the feeling of their parts that they can carry on a private conversation between the lines. On the other hand Rotrou's *Saint Genest* postulates an actor so deeply immersed in his role that he becomes completely identified with it and assumes it as his own nature: Genesius, burlesquing a Christian, becomes a Christian in mid-performance. This of course is a special case, but to make sense at all it must correspond to some known pattern of stage behaviour. For lack of detailed evidence, we can only offer a generalisation: that although some actors were more deeply involved in their roles than others, for the most part tragic acting was a highly studied performance, extrovert rather than introspective. It could none the less have enormous power when done well and played before an audience accustomed to the conventions.

Equally obviously, it could decay into affectation, exaggeration and mindless posturing, providing the parodists with an easy target. Any formal style of acting presents the same problems. A good actor can use the conventions and make them work for him. An inferior actor may be dominated by them, and go through the motions of the performance without comprehending its essence. An acting style as far removed from everyday life as the one we are now considering could easily degenerate into mannerism and absurdity. We hear, for example, of one actress so uninvolved in the words she was speaking that she played every part, however tragic, with a fixed smile. Molière clearly believed that tragedy should be played on a more human note, and has left us valuable information about the absurdities he professed to find in his rivals. In *L'Impromptu de Versailles* he aims the following parody at the noted tragedians of the Hôtel de Bourgogne:

I had an inspiration for a comedy. It would have a playwright in it (that would be my part) who'd come to offer his play to a company just arrived from the provinces. 'Do you have actors and actresses', he'd ask them, 'capable of performing a work as it deserves? Because my play is one that –' 'Sir' the actors would reply to him, 'we have ladies and gentlemen who've been well enough received in every place we went to on our tour.' 'All right. Which of you plays the kings?' 'The actor over there. He plays them sometimes.' 'What! That good-looking youngster? You must be joking! A king should be a big man, as fat as four people put together! Heavens above, a king should have a proper belly on him! A king should possess an enormous circumference, so that he can fill a throne as it needs to be filled! What, cast a strapping young lad like that as a king? That's your first big mistake. But let me hear you recite a dozen lines or so.' Then the actor would recite, say, some of the king's lines from *Nicomède*:

'What can I say, Araspes? He has served me all too well,
Increasing my dominions...'

in the most natural tone possible. Then the playwright says 'What! You call that acting! Nonsense! You have to come down heavy on the words. Listen.' (He imitates Montfleury, the actor at the Hôtel de Bourgogne.) 'You see this pose? Note it well. Bring out the last line good and strong. That always goes down well with the audience. They'll give you a big hand.' 'But, sir,' the actor would reply, 'it seems to me that if the king was having a private conversation with his captain of the guard, he'd talk more like an ordinary human being, not rant and rave like a monster.' 'That shows how much you know! You just wait and see! If you speak the lines the way you're doing now, you won't raise so much as a murmur from the audience.'

Molière's rivals were not slow to reply. The son of the abused Montfleury (who was, in fact, immensely fat) wrote a satire called *L'Impromptu de l'Hôtel de Condé*, which ridiculed Molière's own tragic style. The speaker compares him to a frozen figure in a tapestry:

That's just how he enters, his nose tilted high,
His shoulder thrust forward, his feet spread awry;
His wig, which wobbles to match his advance,
Is stuck fuller with bayleaves than ham from Mayence.
His hands hug his hips, rather carefree and cool,
And he pulls back his head like a loaded-down mule.
Then, eyes rolling wild, he commences his speech
One word at a time, with a 'hic' between each.

Cruel, and perhaps even true. The description matches a familiar portrait of Molière bewigged and laurel crowned in Corneille's *The*

Death of Pompey. We have to make allowance for professional jealousy. 'Why don't the Bourgogne actors send up Molière's company?' runs one contemporary joke. 'Because they could never be such bad actors!' Even so, it seems fairly clear that Molière could be faulted for failing to achieve the same style whose excesses he criticised in others, and that his attempted reforms of the heavy tragic manner were either misunderstood or rejected by audiences happy with the old ways. Although Molière, like most actors, began by playing both tragedy and comedy, he seems to have been sensitive to the ridicule he received. 'At the Hôtel de Bourgogne.' says one critic, 'I only laugh at the comedies. When I see Molière's company I laugh at the tragedies too.' And so Molière found others to replace him in his tragic roles, and concentrated increasingly, and finally exclusively, on comedy, where his true genius lay.

A great deal of what we know of comic acting at this time also comes largely from other people's descriptions of Molière, though in this case the descriptions are more sympathetic. Even in the mouths of his worst enemies, one can detect a grudging regard for his amazing physical stamina and versatility. His critics could only try to denigrate this by asserting that it derived not from natural genius but from his ability to mimic good models. *Singe* is an epithet used frequently of actors at this time, but particularly of Molière: monkey see, monkey do. (It did not help that he was born in a house decorated with a carved frieze of monkeys.) He had learned from others, clearly, but had learned well – particularly from the Italian players whose traditional, highly physical farce was so popular in Paris, and most of all from Tiberio Fiorilli, the most celebrated Italian performer of his time.

So far we have talked of actors and playwrights who were seen to be constantly busy, always in demand; whose performances were sponsored by the highest ranks of French society; and whose offerings were eagerly discussed and minutely dissected. There has surely never been another society which lavished so much critical attention on the output of the theatre. Every educated member of the audience, from the newly formed Académie Française downwards, seemed determined to intrude his words of praise or blame. Everyone, it seemed was a critic; and though this had its bad side in the formation of cliques and cabals, and sporadic hate-campaigns against particular works or authors, it invested every new production, and every acting début, with an aura of excitement from which the theatre as an institution could only profit.

There was, however, another aspect of theatrical life. In this age, side by side with the critical esteem, we find an amplified form of that love–hate relationship that the public has always had with those who pursue the stage as a career. On the surface, it might seem that the profession was now socially secure. By royal edict, actors were respectable members of society and no longer the outcasts they had clearly been in other times and places. Officially, a woman no longer forfeited her respectability by appearing on the stage. But the practice belied the theory. Such pronouncements, even from the highest sources, could not eradicate the vast groundswell of public opinion, the rooted traditional prejudice, aided and abetted by the Church, which persisted in regarding the theatre as socially and morally suspect. From the earliest history of the theatre this prejudice, though varying in degree, has remained the same in kind. Amateur acting has always been tolerated, as long as its practitioners have a respectable occupation in ordinary life. Thus it was no conceivable degradation for Louis XIV to take featured roles in court ballets, for the pupils of the Jesuit schools to appear in classical plays, or for the cloistered schoolgirls of St Cyr to stage a tragedy by Racine. But any attempt to make a living by such means has always called forth the disapproval of the moralists. From Greek times on, the tone of protest has remained the same. To act a role is to present a lie, and is therefore morally reprehensible. To engage in a function which has no permanent, useful product is to oppose oneself to all honest workers and tradesmen. This fundamental hostility is still apparent in our own time; in France of the seventeenth century, it was particularly virulent.

Thus we have the ambiguity. On the one hand favoured performers might enjoy official and public adulation and pursue their careers without stigma to a monetary and social reward. Molière was permitted to continue in his royal appointment. Floridor the actor, and Jean Baptiste Lully the composer and ballet-master, were allowed to enrol themselves among the nobility, and both died wealthy and esteemed men. On the other hand the profession as a whole, particularly in its lower reaches, was subject to abuse and innuendo. Some of this was ecclesiastically inspired. The Church could hardly take a united stand against the theatre, for the two cardinal-ministers, Richelieu and Mazarin, had been notable patrons of the arts, and other prominent clerics found themselves honestly unable to condemn the stage as such. But there was pronounced hostility on the part of others, a residuum of the long antagonism between Church and stage which dated from the first Christian protests against the burlesquing of their religion in the Roman theatre. The condemnation of Roman mimes by the fathers of the Church could still be quoted by French abbés against the Hôtel de Bourgogne and the Palais Royal.

Individual harassment could be severe. There is some reason to believe that Molière's Illustre Théâtre failed in part because it was located in a parish whose priest was notoriously hostile to the drama. The *cause célèbre* of *Tartuffe*, denounced from the archiepiscopal pulpit because of its supposed heresies, shows how savage such feeling could be; and in the period after Molière's death his actors found it almost impossible to relocate themselves in a Paris where every parish seemed to bar its doors against them. The moral opposition is most succinctly formulated by the Prince de Conti, a recusant patron of the drama, whose *Treatise on the Theatre according to the Traditions of the Church* (1666) contains the following terse, damning, and, to many, unarguable statement: 'Between the theatre, whose object is to arouse the passions, and Christianity, whose object is to calm them, subjugate them and – in so far as is possible in this life – destroy them, there is total opposition.'

Taking its tone from such strictures, popular gossip delighted in weaving scurrilous fantasies around actors' private lives. Again, Molière's career may be used as an index of his times. He was particularly prone to attack in reprisal for the attacks, real or imaginary, that he made on others; scarcely one of his plays went by without some individual objecting that he had been personally lampooned by the author. Thus private resentment and public prurience combined to make Molière the target of almost unbelievably vicious gossip. He was accused of both incest and homosexuality – the former with his young wife Armande alleged to be his own daughter by his former mistress Madeleine, and the latter with the actor Michel Baron, whom another stream of gossip represented as Armande's lover. The charge of incest is interesting because it appears to have been started by Molière's old enemy, the tragic actor Montfleury, and to have provoked reaction on the highest level. Louis XIV himself lent his weight to the clearing of Molière's name by standing as godfather to his firstborn, and banning a slanderous publication on the subject. There is certainly some small doubt as to who Armande was, and modern scholars have pursued the issue with scarcely less relish than the seventeenth-century gossips. She may have been Madeleine's younger sister, as documentary evidence seems to indicate, though this would make her mother suspiciously old for childbirth. She may have been Madeleine's daughter, but by another lover. Molière's friends and supporters repudiated the charge as eagerly as it was advocated by his enemies, and there seems to be no real evidence for it. But the fact that such a story could come into existence at all testifies to the low esteem in which actors were held. Even after Molière's death, when Armande was left to manage the company, she was not let alone. A vicious pamphlet, *La Fameuse Comédienne* – anonymous, perhaps written by some disgruntled actor – raked up the old rumours and scandals; and it evidently found a good reading public.

The events of Molière's death are equally indicative, revealing as they do the hazards to which actors were subject when royal favour could no longer protect them. His last performance, on 17 February, 1673, was ironically in his own *The Imaginary Invalid*. Immediately afterwards he collapsed and had to taken home to bed. Priests were summoned, but could not, or would not come, and at ten in the evening he died without the final blessing of the Church. Since he had failed to earn grace by formally renouncing his profession, he was classed with Jews, infidels and excommunicants and refused burial in consecrated soil; his body was laid to rest at first above ground level. It took a petition to the King to secure a decent burial, and even this was carried out grudgingly, at night, with a minimum of ceremony.

Thus passed a man whose career is the epitome of the theatre of his time: a theatre touched with greatness, which rose from humble, nomadic beginnings to rub shoulders with the mighty of the land, to become the focus of the intellectual and the fashionable world; a theatre which could wear fine clothes, but which still trailed its feet in the mud. Nor does the story end with Molière. In the next century Adrienne Lecouvreur, the most famous actress of the Comédie Française, idolised in her lifetime, was flung out on a garbage heap after her death. It has been, and probably will be, ever thus.

4 The Conditions of Tragedy

In the modern theatre the critic, whether he likes it or not, plays a secondary role. His function is to comment after the dramatic event, to evaluate the dramatist's achievement in the light of his intentions, and to recreate for the reader the experience of the audience in the theatre. He does not, as a rule, suggest ways in which the dramatist may next proceed; he may define trends, he may occasionally predict them, but he does not dictate them; and though his influence may be powerful, indeed crucial, it is normally exercised with respect to work already done, and not work yet to come. The dramatist, similarly, would react with hostility to any suggestion that the pattern of his play should be predetermined by someone else. If he conforms to established modes of playwriting it is more likely to be for commercial than for critical reasons.

In the seventeenth century the case was different. The critic saw himself not as a reviewer – though every play of note was analysed in detail after its first performance – but as a theorist, whose prime function was to establish standards, suggest models, and lay down lines along which the drama might usefully proceed. We must remember too that we are dealing with France, a country which has consistently sought to regulate its language and literature with a severity unknown elsewhere. The Académie Française was called into being to define academic standards whereby literary achievement could be measured (although, as modern writers have pointed out, the history of French literature can be written from the names of those who were never elected to the Académie). Only the French would have laboured for so many years over a monumental dictionary of approved usage. French ministries send out a stream of bulletins designed to combat the creeping menace of *franglais* and protect the purity of the language, even in its modern technological vocabulary, from Anglo-American importations. Preservation societies guard literary works as jealously as if they were threatened buildings; in the 1960s a film of *Les Liaisons Dangereuses* was denied an export licence because it was considered to be a travesty of the original novel, so that its showing might diminish French cultural prestige abroad.

It is in this context that we must see the writing of the French tragedy. Critics conceived it as their duty to set standards and apply them. Dramatists were for the most part happy to conform, or at the least to publish a reasoned defence of their departure from established principles. Most of the major tragedies of this period were accompanied in print by a copious self-critique, establishing the sources from which the author had drawn his play and explaining his own working methods. Nor did playwrights feel themselves debased by this relinquishment of autonomy. In a rationalist age, they were content to agree that there should be rules in the theatre just as in every other aspect of an ordered life. In any case, the desire for originality is a comparatively recent artistic phenomenon. It was the Romantics who first, towards the end of the eighteenth century, saw novelty as in itself desirable. The same age that liberated the individual from traditional political systems freed the artist from established critical systems; the Romantics went out of their way to write the previously unwritten, to break the rules, to cultivate change for the sake of change. Earlier writers were happier when they could borrow distinction for their work by attaching it to an established tradition, and by seeking out prestigious models.

Circumstances conspired to present French tragedians with a particular set of models drawn from Greek and Roman antiquity. Rediscovered by the Renaissance, disseminated by the new art of printing and studied eagerly throughout Europe, these works had reminded the world of a type of drama that the Middle Ages had either forgotten or preserved only in distorted memory. Their theatrical impact had already been considerable. To a society seeking rules and standards, their dramatic power, economy of means and clarity of expression had an undeniable attraction. Nor was this attraction entirely literary. Contemporary political theory, which sought to affirm the King not merely as the supreme head of state but of the Catholic Church in France also, turned naturally to Rome as an exemplar. No visitor to Versailles can fail to have been struck by the statue of Louis XIV in the dress of a Roman emperor. Richelieu had consciously advocated the Roman view of literature and the arts as an arm of government and an instrument of national prestige. By the time of the full flowering of the French drama, we are talking of a society permeated with classical thought, and subscribing to the classical view of the world as one in which there was an ultimate order, discernible by reason though liable to disruption by the passions. We see the manifestations of this ideal in society and the arts:

codification, regularity, symmetry, order, proportion, balance. And we see, in consequence, the natural adoption of Greek and Roman models, in the theatre as in all things else. Racine writes tragedies based on Euripides; Molière composes comedies after Plautus and Terence; Boileau presents a critical treatise in verse, *L'Art Poétique*, frankly modelled on the *Ars Poetica* of Horace.

The writers of the seventeenth century had access to more or less the same body of classical literature that we do now. They knew much less about the everyday lives of the ancients, for the great archaeological discoveries which would illuminate such matters were still far in the future, and this may have contributed to a tendency to idealise the past. But at least they had most of the works; few new discoveries have been made since their time, and these have been of comparatively minor significance. Although the classical plays were known, however, they were not known in the same degree to everyone – sometimes only at second hand, sometimes imperfectly understood. It was some time before Greek became a normal university subject, and the Jesuits were primarily Latinists. Not every writer had Racine's facility with Greek in the original. But French translations of Greek and Roman works had begun to appear in the sixteenth century, and Seneca's Latin adaptations of Greek tragedy were accessible to anyone with a good orthodox education. Thus the general outline of classical drama was well enough understood, and we must ask now to what extent this outline was followed.

Firstly, subject matter. The Greeks and their Roman imitators had restricted themselves, partly by tradition and partly by design, to a limited range of stories culled from the more familiar myths and legends. This range must originally have been larger than what we now see, for much of the material has been lost to us. Nevertheless it is obvious that certain groups of stories, such as the misfortunes of the doomed houses of Agamemnon or Oedipus, had a perennial appeal and lost nothing in the retelling. The same material served a succession of dramatists, with minor variations of plot but substantial differences of interpretation. Much of the interest, for Greek audiences, lay in comparing versions and matching each new treatment of a given story against its predecessors.

In this respect French tragedy offers no real comparison, for the neo-classic writers permitted themselves a much wider range of subjects. It is true, of course, that a number of French plays, including some of the most famous, were modelled directly on Greek and Roman originals, and that some subjects were particularly popular. Corneille wrote a

Medea, and Racine left notes for one; Racine wrote several plays inspired by Euripidean models, and one of the most celebrated controversies of the century erupted in 1677 when, within three days, both Racine and his rival Pradon brought out tragedies based on Euripides' *Hippolytus.*

There were, however, other rich and popular sources of subject matter. Following the example of Jodelle, whose *Cléopâtre Captive* (1552) set a number of patterns for the later age, French playwrights roamed widely through the profitable fields of Greek and Roman history. Racine set one play in the Indian campaigns of Alexander the Great. Du Ryer turned to the struggles of the early Roman Republic for *Scévole* (*Scaevola*) as did Corneille for *Horace* (*Horatius*). The Roman Empire gave Racine his *Britannicus,* based on an episode in the reign of Nero, whose complex and sinister personality has always attracted dramatists; though Titus, a 'good' emperor, inspired no fewer than three plays. Magnon's *Titus* (1660), Corneille's *Titus and Berenice* (1670), and Racine's *Bérénice* in the same year. The troubled history of Christianity under the late Empire gave Corneille his *Polyeucte* and Rotrou his *Saint Genest,* both stories of Christian martyrdom. Tristan l'Hermite's *Les Malheurs domestiques du Grand Constantin* (*The Unhappy Private Life of Constantine the Great*) found sensational material in the dynastic squabbles surrounding the first Christian Emperor.

But there were many plays whose subject matter owed nothing to classical antiquity. Some were biblical in inspiration, like Tristan's *Mariane,* whose rigours did such harm to Montdory, or Racine's last two works for the stage, *Esthère* and *Athalie.* Some were Spanish, like Corneille's *Le Cid.* And there is a whole string of plays, beginning with Bounyn's *The Sultana* in 1560, which turned to the exotic East, and particularly to the lurid politics of the Turkish court: Mainfroy's *The Girl from Rhodes,* or *The Cruelty of Soliman* (1620); Mairet's *Soliman* or *The Death of Mustapha* (1630); Le Voyer's *Selim the Great,* or *The Tragic Coronation;* Jacquelin's *Solyman,* or *The Generous Slave-girl* (1653). The French, secure in their self-imposed order, looked with fascinated horror on the blood-splattered history of the Turkish dynasties, with their assassinations, mutilations and palace revolutions. 'How different, how very different,' we can almost hear them murmuring, 'from the home life of our own dear King;' and they attended such spectacles on the stage as eagerly as they read of them in broadsheets or the foreign mail. It would not be too much of an exaggeration to say that *turquerie* was to the seventeenth century what *chinoiserie* was to the eighteenth; and even *chinoiserie* appears in the drama, though late, with Regnard and Dufresny's *The Chinese* in 1692.

In subject matter, then, there is no real comparison between the Greek drama and the French. In the mechanics of putting a play together, the debt is more obvious. Greek tragedy was characterised by its supreme dramatic economy, and could speak to powerful effect with the minimum of physical means. The plays were written for a maximum of three speaking actors, and though each actor could play multiple roles, and non-speaking extras could be added at will, the practical effect of this restriction was that no scene could involve more than three speaking characters at a time. French tragedy adhered to this restriction in spirit, though it did not follow it to the letter. Cast-lists still tended to be short (compare the demands of French tragedy to those of Elizabethan or Jacobean plays) and the number of major characters was more restricted still; we have seen in the case of the Marais how a small company could handle most of the plays it would be called upon to perform. Such limitations could, however, pose problems for egotistical actors, whose contracts might include, as a fringe benefit, the first choice of roles. In terms of dramatic action, the restricted cast necessitated a play that proceeded mainly by soliloquies and dialogues. Racine is the supreme master of this kind of dramatic economy. His crucial scenes normally involve two people only. Only rarely do we find a more complex staging such as the end of Act Three of his *Phèdre*, where Thésée asks his angry, baffled questions of a Hippolyte who refuses to give a straight answer and a Phèdre, supported physically and spiritually by Oenone, who can hardly speak at all.

The Greeks had another casting restriction that French did not inherit: the insistence on an all-male ensemble. In Greece, this had been an inevitable product of the social situation. In a culture where women were at best second-class citizens, it was inconceivable that they should participate in one of the most important civic and religious celebrations of the state. All women's roles were therefore written to be played by men, a fact which explains the strong masculinity of most female protagonists in Greek tragedy. This did not apply in France, where the use of actresses had been known since the Middle Ages and encouraged by the visits of Italian companies. By the seventeenth century French audiences were well accustomed to seeing women on the stage, in sharp contrast to England, which did not see its first actress until after the Restoration. In French comedy the older transvestite tradition was still occasionally observed – the role of Mme Jourdain, in Molière's *Le Bourgeois Gentilhomme*, was created by the actor Hubert – but in tragedy Racine's Andromache was played by a woman where Euripides' character had been taken by a man. There was thus a greater and

more subtle awareness of feminine psychology on the stage, which
manifested itself in the growing complexity and sophistication of
women's roles.

In another respect, however, French tragedy restricted itself much
more severely than the Greek by eliminating the chorus. In Greek
tragedy the chorus had several functions. As characters its members
could act as interlocutors in the drama, addressing the principal characters, responding to them, and helping to forward the plot. But they
could also step outside the immediate action and comment upon it,
drawing a moral from the previous scene or enlarging upon it and linking it to the wider world of the audience's experience. Their song and
dance also contributed a spectacular dimension to the performance of
Greek drama which we can never fully recover, for we have lost the
original music and with it the Greek sense of the harmony of physical
movement and the spoken word.

French dramatists never fully explored the use of the chorus, and
their reluctance to do so owes as much to architectural and economic
factors as to any cultural change. The Greek chorus demanded space in
which to manoeuvre and uninhibited access to its audience. In the
characteristic Greek theatre structure both of these demands were met.
The audience surrounded the action, and the chorus, both literally and
figuratively, bridged the gap between the public and the play. In the
French theatre this spatial expansiveness was lost. Audiences were
accustomed to a different kind of theatre structure, and Greek choruses,
as modern directors know to their cost, cannot happily be adapted to a
proscenium stage. Greek tragedy drew strength from the free communication between the play and its audience, which was harangued, cajoled
and stimulated by choric dances drawing on familiar ritual patterns to
compel an emotional surrender. In the French theatre this sense of communion was lost when the drama came indoors. The proscenium arch
created a barrier between the audience and the action, and the public,
once a participant, was now reduced to the status of a spectator. In a
theatre where the Greek forms of communication were denied, the Greek
chorus had no place.

The economics of the theatre had also changed. Greek choruses were
drawn from volunteer, unpaid members of the citizen body. The French
theatre used paid professionals, with the consequent necessity of keeping
the companies as small as possible. In addition it may be remarked that
the classical authors who most influenced French tragedy were not
Aeschylus and Sophocles, for whom the chorus was vital, but Euripides
and, after him, Seneca. In Euripides' plays the chorus had already yielded

pride of place to the actors, and by Seneca's time did little more than provide lyric interludes between scenes.

All these factors combined to eliminate the chorus from the French theatre. It appeared in some of the early plays, which were more clearly intended as academic reconstructions, but even here was used in the debased Senecan manner, as a formal observance of ancient proprieties rather than an organic part of the drama. The commercial theatre found no use for the chorus in tragedy. Racine returned to it for his last two plays, but these were a special case: Esthère and Athalie were written for private performance at a fashionable girls' school, where actresses did not have to be paid and there was every inducement, as in any amateur performance, to provide parts for as many people as possible. (Though Racine, it must be noted, claimed more honourable motives: 'to effect a union, as in ancient Greek tragedy, between the choral song and the action, and to use the chorus, which the pagans had employed to sing the praises of their false divinities, to sing instead the praises of the One True God.')

Yet although the chorus for all practical purposes disappeared, its various functions were absorbed in other ways. The role of interlocutor was now taken by minor characters in the play. In French tragedy the principal characters are regularly provided with friends and confidants who act as sounding-boards for their opinions, draw them out and offer them advice. In the lists of *dramatis personae* names are neatly paired off, each principal with a subordinate, and the confidant becomes a familiar and useful, though eventually overworked, convention.

The extent to which the confidant takes over this function of the choral role may best be seen by comparison. Euripides' *Hippolytus* introduces the principal characters by means of a double chorus. First we have a chorus of huntsmen, singing the praises of the goddess Artemis and the delights of the chase, to which Hippolytus is addicted. There follows a dialogue between Hippolytus himself and an old servant, who warns him that if he continues to show excessive devotion to one deity while ignoring the rest, he may be in for trouble. Then the main chorus enters, composed of women of the palace. They sing a vivid description of Queen Phaedra's mysterious malady, speculating on its origins but finding no answer. When Phaedra enters in her old nurse's arms, the women urge the nurse to question her mistress, and in the ensuing scene the dreadful secret is revealed: Phaedra is in love with her own stepson. In Racine's version there is no chorus, but the same material is covered by the characters alone. The play opens with a dialogue between Hippolyte and his confidant Theramène, in which the prince's basic character is revealed. Oenone, Phèdre's lady-in-waiting, enters, with a short speech describing the Queen's illness. Phèdre then appears, delirious; and Oenone's sympathy turns to a curiosity which eventually probes the true cause.

Some vestige of the spectacular function of the Greek chorus also remained, but not in tragedy. It resided in a distinct art form, the ballet, which was sung as well as danced and took many of its themes from classical mythology. Some critics even professed to find ballet the superior art, and a more sensitive recreation of the spirit of ancient drama than tragedy could ever be; as we shall see in a later chapter, they were able to quote supportive argument from the ancients themselves. We may add here the 'machine plays', the massive musical spectacles which were a by-product of ballet and used large singing and dancing choruses to great effect; like ballet too, they drew much of their material from classical mythology. There is no Greek chorus in Corneille's *Medea*, but there is at least an approximation to Greek choral spectacle in the same author's *La Conquête de la Toison d'Or* (*The Capture of the Golden Fleece*). The one function of the Greek chorus which completely disappears is its use as a discursive, disembodied voice to comment on the events of the drama and place them in a wider frame of reference. For this we have to wait until the adaptations of Greek drama offered by French writers in the twentieth century: Cocteau's *La Machine Infernale* (*The Infernal Machine*) with its prologue broadcast over a loudspeaker, or Anouilh's *Antigone* with its solo chorus describing the characters and what is to happen to them.

In seeking to define other key elements of the classical drama that they could adapt or imitate, French playwrights could look not only at the tragedies themselves but at various critical studies that had been written on them. In some respects this was a mixed blessing. We have little criticism contemporary with the period in which Aeschylus, Sophocles and Euripides were writing, and what there is concerns itself more with the social function of the theatre than with artistic principles of dramatic composition. In his comedy *The Frogs* (405 B.C.) Aristophanes stages a debate between Aeschylus and Euripides, whom he identifies as polar opposites in their attitudes toward the writing and performance of tragedy. Although much of the supposed criticism in this play is merely frivolous, one point is amply and seriously made: that in Greek eyes the playwright had a duty to advise and educate his audience. Drama, in a word should be committed, and the playwright should function as artist-teacher. This was the prevailing Greek view of any art, at least in fifth-century society: it should be functional and have an end outside itself. Plato accepted this doctrine wholly when he considered the place of drama in his utopian state, and was reluctantly forced to conclude that, if plays did not clearly lead the public into ways of virtue, they did not deserve to exist. His strictures gave ammunition to the opponents of the drama for centuries to come; they were delighted to find that they could quote the Greeks against themselves.

It was left to Aristotle, Plato's fourth-century successor, sometime heir and sometime rival, to write what was, as far as we know, the first critical work to consider drama as an end in itself, divorced from sociological and educational considerations, and to attempt to formulate purely artistic criteria for the composition of plays. This work, the *Poetics*, was the single most powerful influence on French critics and playwrights. For some it was a starting-point, a useful handbook, while for others it became a Bible. Unfortunately our understanding of the *Poetics* has been flawed by time, and it is important at the outset to consider what kind of work it was, what it was trying to do, and what relationship it had to the plays cited in it as examples.

Aristotle, descended from a family of doctors, was a scientist who turned himself into a polymath. His writings embrace almost every serious study of his time: politics, rhetoric, physics, metaphysics (it was Aristotle himself who coined the term metaphysics), ethics, pure science and literature. To all these studies he brought his sound scientific training. He began his work on politics by having his assistants assemble as many examples of different constitutions as they could find – and in Greece, these were many indeed; from these he set out to establish, inductively, the general principles governing politics as a whole. In the same way, when he wrote the *Poetics*, he began with individual plays and, from this evidence, sought to identify the general laws of dramatic composition. It is important to remember that he was writing long after the event. The plays he chose to discuss were the masterpieces of the fifth century, by his time already canonised as 'classics'; although revivals, particularly of Euripides, were frequent, it is doubtful how many of his examples Aristotle could actually have seen on the stage, and the play in performance is a different animal from the play in script form. We may be dealing, then, with a work rather remote from theatrical actuality.

There are other hazards in using the *Poetics*, deriving from the nature of the work itself and the way it has been mutilated by time. As written, it was in three parts, dealing with epic poetry, tragedy and comedy respectively. The study of comedy has vanished completely, leaving a fruitful field for scholars who try to reconstruct the workings of Aristotle's mind. The section on epic has disappeared almost as completely. Even the surviving portion has inherent difficulties. It is written in a curiously dense and cryptic style in which key words, and often extended passages, defy easy comprehension and analysis. Some scholars have sought to explain these difficulties by suggesting that the work was never intended for publication in the form in which we have it. Rather, it may represent Aristotle's lecture notes, designed to be amplified and clarified in class, or even the notes of a pupil attending that class; and lecture notes, whether student's or professor's, are notoriously indecipherable, particularly so long after the event. In evaluating the *Poetics*, therefore, a great burden rests on the interpreter, and the work has generated volumes of commentary out of all proportion to its own length.

Nevertheless the *Poetics* had for other ages the virtue of uniqueness. It was the first and only example of its kind, a study of Greek drama by a Greek still in touch with the great tradition, and for this reason was avidly seized upon by later theorists who sought to distil from it principles which they could apply to the drama of their own time. Italian and French critics laid down their versions of what they thought Aristotle had said, and urged the playwrights to put their theories into practice. In certain key ways the *Poetics* was seen to support the principles of dramatic economy observable in the works themselves, and this had important consequences for the writing and staging of French tragedy.

Aristotle made one important basic observation about the tragic plot. The story, he suggested, should properly concern itself with a single issue, and refrain from straying into byways and irrelevancies. From the plays themselves we can see that this is generally true. Although the associations conjured up by the action of Greek tragedy may be complex and far-reaching, the action itself is usually a simple one, expressible in a single sentence. Oedipus seeks the murderer of Laius and finds it is himself. Orestes murders his mother in vengeance for his father's death. There is no room for the subplots and complexity of issues that we observe in Elizabethan drama. The critics who rediscovered Aristotle in the Renaissance took this suggestion and elevated it to the precept later defined as the Unity of Action. French dramatists accepted the strength of this simplicity and more or less happily conformed to it. This automatically created a gulf between the French and the English dramatic tradition. Though both shared common patterns in the Middle Ages, the English remained discursive and expansive, while the French became taut and compressed. French critics professed themselves unable to come to terms with Shakespeare unless he was adapted to conform with classical principles; French audiences hardly saw Shakespeare in un-mutilated form until the Romantics, rebelling against their own tradi-tion, rediscovered him and made him their god.

Another of Aristotle's suggestions was just as readily accepted, though perhaps on less valid authority. He observes that the action of Greek tragedy usually takes place 'in one revolution of the sun'. In other words, dramatic time is approximate to real time; the Greeks do not write plays like Marlowe's *Doctor Faustus*, in which the action stretches over twenty-four years, or Shakespeare's *Julius Caesar*, where months of historical time are compressed into three hours. The Greeks did not regard the limitation of time as a hard-and-fast rule. Aeschylus' *Oresteia* trilogy covers the history of centuries, from the end of the Trojan War to the establishment of the first criminal court in Athens, in a story of two generations, and even within the limits of individual plays time may be considered flexible if this suits the dramatic purpose: in *Agamemnon* the news of Troy's fall is brought first by a chain of beacon-fires and almost immediately afterwards by a herald who has come by sea, a voyage which should logically have taken considerably longer. Other plays which ostensibly adhere to a straightforward time-scheme are free to compress or extend time in matters of detail and background. But on the whole Aristotle's observation is sound. Most plays operate like Euripides' *Bacchae*, where the whole action unfolds in a few hours in front of the royal palace.

Once again, the later critics took this observation and turned it into a law. There was some unprofitable argument about whether 'one revolution of the sun' meant twelve hours or twenty-four. One critic advocated the former, on the grounds that nothing of much dramatic importance happens after dark. A rival critic disagreed. On the contrary, he argued; much of mankind's most important activity takes place by night. After the bickering was over, French tragedy settled down with the Unity of Time, accepting that the action of a drama should occupy, more or less, the span of one full day. Racine's *Phèdre* begins with the protagonist crying for the rising sun, and ends amid references to the shining stars. The more exuberant dramatists occasionally found this restriction irksome. Corneille's *Le Cid* packed so much activity into a single day that the author was censured, not for breaking the rules, but for keeping them in such a way as to make them ridiculous. But most writers were prepared to recognise a circumscribed period of activity, and confine themselves to dramatic events that might reasonably and plausibly occur within the limits suggested.

To these two 'unities' was added a third, this time clearly based on a misunderstanding of Greek practice. This was the Unity of Place, which prescribed that each play should confine itself to one location, with the action never moving beyond these self-appointed limits. As with the Unity of Time, this may seem to be true of Greek tragedy, but in fact is only partially and superficially true. Certainly Aeschylus sets the whole of *Agamemnon* in front of the royal palace at Argos, and Prometheus is bound to his rock for the length of the play; all the events of *Medea* take place before Medea's house in Corinth, and those of *Oedipus the King* before the palace of Thebes. But these examples should not blind us to the no less important exceptions. In other plays the scenic location can change, in major or in subtle ways. In the *Eumenides* we move from Delphi to Athens, and then to various places within Athens; in *Ajax* from the hero's tent to a remote spot on the seashore; in *Hecuba* ambiguously from one shore to another, whichever is more dramatically convenient at the time. Convenience, in fact, appears to be the operative word. The Greek theatre, with its neutral and scenically undefined acting space, presented the audience with a void that had to be filled and coloured by the dialogue. Characters tell us where they are, and what the setting is supposed to be. If this is unimportant to the action, they do not bother to tell us. Sometimes the story was such that it demanded some specific location, usually a house, a temple or a palace. In these cases the permanent architectural background of the theatre could serve to represent such structures as were necessary, and be given a specific identification by the actor's words. But when the story-line required a shift, the setting could immediately be redefined by the poet's language and the actions of his characters, and the architectural background imagined out of sight at need. The Greek stage setting, existing largely in the mind, was therefore infinitely flexible, and could be changed at will.

To this extent, then, the neoclassical 'unity of place' represents a constriction of the imagination, though it may be more charitable to see it as a compromise between ancient modes of thought and more recent modes of staging. The Greek audience was embraced within the action as a willing partner, lending its creative imagination to the accomplishment of the dramatic act. The French audience was distanced from the action by barriers both physical and psychological and asked not to be a participant in a common rite but to observe, at some remove, a moving, talking picture. By force of theatrical circumstances the French took one of the several possibilities offered by Greek scenic practice and established it as their norm.

Even within this norm, however, there was still room for variation, and some playwrights came near to the Greek imaginative flexibility. For Corneille, in *Le Cid*, the proprieties are preserved if all the scenes are located reasonably close together:

> All the action takes place in Seville, and thus preserves some kind of Unity of Place overall, but the particular place of action changes from one scene to another. At one time it is the palace of the King, at another the Infanta's private chamber, at another Chimène's house, at another some street or public place.

Corneille envisages a 'poetic fiction' whereby one scene may merge insensibly into another. A conversation started on the threshold of the King's palace turns to a quarrel as the speakers pass through the street; provocation is offered, and the injured party withdraws into his house to seek recourse. The action is continuous but the place is assumed to change, and we are obviously close to the old Greek freedom here. This has been intelligently realised in the modern production at the Comédie Française by a neutral setting of tarnished golden grilles which may equally well signify inside or outside, and assume whatever specific identity the action gives them.

Even where the scene is more rigidly defined, there may still be room for the same convenient ambiguity. This is true, for example, in Racine's *Phèdre*. As the play opens the overwhelming impression is that we are in the open air. Phèdre, sick with her secret passion for her stepson, has demanded fretfully to be brought out of doors. Oenone, her lady-in-waiting, reports:

> Torn by her fitful temper from her bed
> She cries for daylight, bidding me to keep
> All people from her melancholy path.

Then Phèdre herself:

> No further, Oenone, let us stay here.
> I cannot stand, my strength is failing me,
> The daylight blinds my eyes, my legs
> Are trembling, giving beneath me.

To which Oenone:

> Now see how one wish wars against another.
> It was you recalled your former strength, and wanted
> To see the daylight, and be seen again.
> And now you see it, do you wish to hide,
> And hate the light you came out here to find?

The impression, furthered by Phèdre's cries at the sun, is immediate and obvious. She stands defenseless in the open light of day, with the sun revealing her shame to the world. But later in the play we have an equally strong sense of the walls closing in, constricting, suffocating. When Phèdre reveals her feelings after her husband's return, we are surely intended to be indoors.

> I know my passion, have it constantly
> Before my mind. These walls, these vaulted roofs
> Already seem as if they would give tongue
> As my accusers, and are only waiting
> Until my husband comes to undeceive him.

We have no contemporary pictorial evidence to resolve this scenic ambiguity, for the original decor of *Phèdre* has been lost. Our earliest illustrations date from the eighteenth century. But perhaps the setting for the first production was a compromise. We have a suggestion of this in the frontispiece to the collected works of Pradon, Racine's contemporary and rival, who wrote his own play on the same theme. The illustration clearly shows a theatrical setting. We see a long, vaulted arcade admitting daylight between the supporting columns at each side, and opening at the rear onto a splendid vista of the seashore, with spires and turrets dimly visible in the distance. Within the gallery, drawing the eye, is a statue of Venus. This was presumably the set for Pradon's play, and so may give us some idea of how Racine's must have looked, with a combination of indoors and outdoors, sunlight and shadow, open vistas and a *palais voûté*.

In many cases, however, the *décor unique* is interpreted rigidly as a single room, framed by wing-pieces representing the walls and closed off by a backdrop, within the confines of which the entire action takes place. Into this room the characters come; here they meet and talk; from here they go to their appointed destinies. Such a restriction requires adroit manipulation of the plot, and dramatists are occasionally heavy-handed in the contrivances that they invent to bring the characters together. There is an amusing example of this kind of manipulation in Tristan l'Hermite's *Le Mort de Senèque (The Death of Seneca)*. The action concerns a plot to overthrow the Emperor Nero, and the single setting is a room in Nero's palace. At one point the conspirators assemble to lay their schemes. Surely, says one of them, this is a dangerous place for us to meet. No, replies another, this is the last place that Nero would think of looking for us.

But in skilful hands the limitation is transformed into an asset. Perhaps the best example is Racine's *Bérénice*, an almost actionless play by some dramatic standards but continually exciting because the prospect of violence is always imminent, though it never materialises. *Bérénice* is a play in five acts about a man making up his mind; and since the man is Titus, Emperor of Rome, his decision is of enormous consequence. Titus it torn between his duty to his people, as their emperor, and his personal inclinations as a man. He is in love with Berenice, the queen of one of Rome's satellite kingdoms. To marry her would threaten the political stability of the Empire. What is he to do? In a room in Berenice's palace, the *décor unique*, the meetings and confrontations leading up to his decision are acted out. The room becomes the still centre of the controversy, the quiet eye of the storm, round which enormous issues are whirling.

The moment of decision comes in Act IV, scene eight. Titus stands in the room. On one side is the door leading to Berenice's chamber, where the Queen is threatening to die for love of him. On the other side is the door beyond which the Roman Senate waits. The crisis is crystallised in a physical decision, brought to sharp focus by the simplicity of the physical surroundings. By choosing a door, Titus chooses a way of life. Reluctantly he decides to go out to his people, and the play can only end on a sigh that such necessities must be.

This apparent sparseness – which is, let us again insist, only apparent – continued to exercise its influence on the French theatre, even in those periods which seemed to owe little to classical influence. Though the Romantics temporarily opened up the stage, the well-made play of the later nineteenth century enclosed it again. The single room with multiple entrances, offering the opportunity for sudden coincidences, chance discoveries and hairsbreadth misses, became the crucible of French farce. Feydeau, hardly less than Racine, acknowledges the utility of the *décor unique*. In our own time Jean-Paul Sartre has rediscovered with brilliant and horrifying effect the values of the single, enclosed space in *Huis Clos* (*Vicious Circle* or *No Exit*) where the three principal characters are isolated in a room in Hell, forced to prey on one another's temperaments and prevented from ever leaving by the unseen menace beyond the doors.

Too often the acceptance of these 'limitations', with their implications, is seen as an act of wilful self-abnegation by the French dramatists, as though they deliberately denied themselves so much of what makes drama rich, vivid and exciting and tried to do their best with what remained. But, in the theatre, we must not confuse economy of means with poverty of expression. Some of the greatest plays have been the simplest: works which, by deliberately restricting their possibilities in some ways, heightened their impact in others by reducing the action to a sharp focus and allowing the imagination to ride free. The French concept of tragedy was a free choice – influenced to some extent by historical and social circumstances, fostered to some extent by theorists and critics, but still a free choice, for valuable and defensible reasons, between the two principal modes of theatre which the Western world had evolved up to that time. The classical mode, as we have seen, was compact and intensive, concentrating on a limited action and a small point in time and from this sharp scrutiny evolving lessons which reverberate through eternity. Medieval drama, in Europe as in England, had sprung from a different source and evolved in contrary ways. Here the inspiring form was the liturgy of the Catholic Church, which was from the beginning a symbolic drama celebrating within the space of less than an hour the life, death and resurrection of Christ. On a larger scale the calendar of the Church year compressed long periods of time into a few months. The festival of Christmas celebrates Christ's birth; three months later Easter week celebrates His passion and resurrection. In addition to this the Old Testament material used in lessons and sermons linked the life of Christ, through the prophetic tradition, to the first manifestations of God's will for mankind. Thus, as the drama of the Christian church evolved, it was able naturally and easily to encompass vast eras of time in a short period of performance, as well as extending its scenic range over every land and culture treated in the biblical narrative. Classical drama considered the moment, and drew lessons for eternity. Medieval drama considered eternity, and drew lessons for the moment.

The medieval religious drama was expansive, multifaceted and episodic. It worked through a succession of short, vivid, self-contained scenes, each with its particular point, though the playlets were responsive to the doctrinal pattern of the cycle as a whole. It embraced a vast number of characters, and often pursued themes that, though largely irrelevant to the religious purpose, were interesting and amusing in their own right. It was from this pattern that the Elizabethan drama, with its large casts, its interweaving of plots and its action wide-roaming in space and extended in time, principally developed. Some Elizabethan dramatists produced their own neo-classical plays, but these were never popular. In the post-Restoration years English writers tried to effect a compromise between native ebullience and classical austerity, but succeeded only in producing a hybrid which enjoyed a short life in the brief glow of fashion. English drama had already made its choice. French drama, in making the opposite choice, denied its medieval heritage and forswore Shakespearean pageantry, but in its espousal of classical simplicity produced a form of tragedy powerful in its own time and scarcely less effective, if approached in the right spirit, in ours.

In considering the effect of these restrictions on French tragedy we should ask not so much what the dramatists did not do as what they did; or rather, how what they did not do affected what they did. It has already been remarked that the omission of part of the dramatic potential induces a concentration on the rest. By paring away side-issues and irrelevant detail we are left with an argument often brutal in its simplicity, revealing itself through a series of stark confrontations. Great passions are set on their collision courses and work upon each other directly. Their energy is not diffused through a multiplicity of persons or subordinate events. In *Macbeth* we trace the effects of Duncan's murder not only on the two participants, but through the ranks of Scottish nobility, the dissolution of the kingdom and the state of nature itself. In *Britannicus* we see the young prince's murder through a few eyes only and are mostly concerned with the murderer, Nero, himself. Shakespeare traces the repercussions and reverberations of the explosion. Racine is concerned with the immediate moment of the explosion itself.

Any explosion has greater force when confined. In this respect the apparent scenic restrictions on tragedy contribute to its power. There are great passions here, and their violence is magnified in a tiny room. French tragedy is, in a valuable sense, claustrophobic. Its characters are confined by social circumstances, by *noblesse oblige*, by traditional concepts of duty and responsibility; within this cage the individual spirit struggles briefly, and often hopelessly, for liberty and the gratification of desire. The characters speak of overwhelming passion but in formal and strictly measured verse, which once again conveys the sense of individual impulse harnessed by traditional restraints, like a mountain torrent flowing between stone banks. This sense of constraint finds its visual counterpart in the limitation of the stage setting. Which comes first, the theatre or the play? It is a chicken-and-egg argument; does the form of the play call a particular form of theatre into being to house it, or does the existing shape of the theatre create a particular form of play? In the French theatre the two things are interdependent. Although the plays of Corneille and Racine have been given in every variety of physical setting, they always seem to demand a proscenium arch, to frame and intensify the action. In the Greek theatre the protagonist's cry spreads out as a ripple of anguish through the universe. In the French, it bounces back from walls and ceiling to fall with redoubled intensity on his own head.

A performance of French tragedy can be an electrifying experience. It is built out of strong passions; of the surging conflicts of strong wills which beat upon, fragment and destroy each other; of the agony of a human need that cannot be reconciled with the dictates of conscience or duty. But the energy is verbal rather than physical. This can pose a problem for the modern theatre, which sets a premium on stage movement, and twentieth-century directors have often attempted to make French tragedy more mobile; there have been productions of Racine in which the violence of the emotions has been realised in physical terms, and characters have literally thrown each other across the stage. In their time, however, the plays eschewed such displays, finding precedents not so much in the Greeks as in Roman standards of dramatic propriety.

Greek tragedy, though largely declamatory, could still embody scenes which had a violent, often horrifying, visual impact. In Sophocles' *Philoctetes* Greek audiences saw a protagonist succumbing to the wrenching agony of his disease, and on two separate occasions writhing in physical torment on the stage. The same author's *Ajax* came near to the visual depiction of suicide, stopping just short of the climactic moment. In *Hecuba* Euripides showed the barbarian Polymestor, newly blinded, crawling like a wounded animal on all fours and groping for the bodies of his murdered children. But even in Greek tragedy, though the scent of death and carnage hangs heavy in the air, the actual moment of death is usually removed from the audience's sight. This was partly due to technical reasons. With only a limited number of performers to divide the roles, an actor who 'died' on stage could not easily return as another character. An off-stage death released the actor, and permitted a dummy to be brought on to represent the corpse. To this extent, then, the avoidance of on-stage death was simply a convenience. But there was also an artistic sensitivity at work which recognised that the description of death or mutilation may be far more horrifying than the visual depiction, because it allows room for the imagination to operate.

Thus, in Greek tragedy, the most violent incidents are never seen. They are anticipated, they are described, and their consequences are explored; only the act itself is concealed from us. The convention of 'messenger's speeches' used to cover such incidents became an integral part of Greek tragedy, and provided actors with some of their most powerful roles. Reported action was preferred to direct action; and there are still audiences who are prepared to swear that they have seen

Oedipus blinding himself, or Pentheus torn apart by the frenzied Bacchae, so forcefully have these descriptions been contrived.

In his *Ars Poetica*, Horace praised this principle on the grounds of artistic propriety. Medea, he observed, should not been seen to kill her children. Such violence should more discreetly happen out of the audience's sight. Seneca's plays, easily accessible to French writers, might seem to belie Horace's theory. These examples of late Roman tragedy are full of the most extraordinary scenes of violence and bloodshed, appropriate to a time when slaughter was considered entertainment, and could be viewed daily in the gladiatorial arena. But these macabre works were probably never intended for full stage performance, and French writers unhesitatingly preferred Horace's chaster prescription. The legacy of medieval drama was discarded. No longer did characters die, bleed or suffer torture and mutilation on the stage. Physical suffering was removed outside the walls of the stage room. Only its repercussions were allowed within. The messenger speech resumed its classical importance.

As in the Greek theatre, part of this reticence must be ascribed to technical causes. Although the enlargement of the cast removed the need to avoid on-stage death scenes, there were still physical constraints upon the action. Stage space was limited, and often encroached upon still further by the audience. There was little room to do much more than stand still and declaim. But from the best of the plays that have survived, we can see how the avoidance of physical action could be translated into a positive virtue. When action is restricted, what remains becomes more meaningful. In Racine, as we have noted, violence is always imminent but rarely physically realised. The constraints of decorum, of propriety, of social circumstance, enforce themselves like tangible bonds upon the characters, so that while they may desire to act, they cannot. In such a context the rare moments of physical contact, though simple in themselves, assume tremendous force, In *Phèdre* there occurs a critical moment when the Queen, having revealed her passion to Hippolyte and been rejected by him, snatches his sword and attempts to plunge it into her breast. It would be a memorable moment in any play. It is doubly so here, because it is the first significant physical action in a play that has already run one third of its course.

The same restraint applies to the more tender emotions. In French tragedy the prime conflict is between duty and desire, love and obligation. Man's rational imperatives are seen to be threatened by the tug of his emotions, and the passion of love most obviously makes war upon the intellect. Characters thus talk eloquently, unendingly, about love, but the talk is never accompanied by love's physical manifestations. They proclaim their passion, but do not touch or embrace. Once again, the physical factors of the performance acquire a thematic importance. Passion may be expressed, but not realised. There is frustration, disappointment; we are left with a view of characters kept apart by forces stronger than themselves.

There were certain other constraints upon French tragedy that were more local and topical, set by the social patterns of the age. In an élitist society it was inevitable that the theatre should pay deference to aristocratic ideals and concern itself with themes and issues of importance to its most prestigious patrons. The power of the monarchy coloured the drama just as it controlled the functions of society, influencing both the subject matter and its treatment. This extended far beyond the occasional obligatory obeisance to the wisdom and virtue of the monarch such as we see, for example, at the end of *Le Cid*, or *Tartuffe*, where the king functions as *deus ex machina* to resolve an apparently insoluble dilemma. From the beginning, it dictated the social level from which the characters of tragedy could acceptably be drawn. Aristotle's dictum that tragedy should deal with people of superior station was translated literally into contemporary social terms to mean kings, queens and the higher ranks of the nobility. French tragedy was class-conscious to a degree. 'I do not number you' says Titus to Antiochus in *Bérénice*, 'among the common rank of kings'; and this is a fair indication of the social level on which tragedy moved, where one virtually had to be a king to begin to play. Even the lesser characters shared in this social advancement. In the Greek theatre, Euripides had been well-known for his democratic attitude towards the personnel of tragedy. His *Medea* opens with a long dialogue between two house-servants, and in *Hippolytus* the most important secondary character is Phaedra's old nurse. In the French theatre this was hardly tolerable. Corneille's *Medea* has parts for Cleone, the governess of the king's daughter, and Theudas, a servant, but these are minimal. In Racine's *Phèdre* the old nurse is promoted, and becomes Oenone, lady-in-waiting at court.

This class-consciousness affects the subject matter of tragedy also. The issues which preoccupy the kings and queens of dramatic fiction tend to be those which revolved about the personality of the ruler in real life. Dramatists were led to investigate the ways in which a monarch functioned, and the extent to which he was able to reconcile his duty to the throne with his personal inclinations. Questions of heredity were good material, because a bad strain in the blood might induce a failure of the royal will at moments of crisis. The matter of legitimate succession was a living issue to an audience concerned with preserving the purity of its own royal line. How are a monarch's decisions made? What kind of opposition does he have to face, and how does he go about overcoming it? To whom does he turn for advice, and what happens if the advice is bad? These are all questions to which French tragedy devoted earnest attention. They were particularly important in a period when the King of France was seen to be susceptible to powerful influences at court, and a word in the royal ear might determine the course of the nation. French tragedy may therefore seem to adopt a critical attitude at times, and even to presume to advise the monarch on the way he is to go. This concern with the substance and show of royalty was therefore not mere snobbishness. The king was important in tragedy because the king was important in life. Again and again in the plays we see the monarch faced with a human decision that assumes momentous significance because he is no longer an ordinary human being. The assumption of kingship requires that he must function on a superior plane; and the friends and confidants who advise him on the basis of their own humanity may unwittingly mislead, because they fail to recognise this fundamental difference.

French tragedy acquired a courtly language appropriate to its subjects. Its vocabulary is formal and restricted. It lacks the explosive vitality that we find in the Elizabethan dramatists, who evolved a dramatic language drawn at once from high poetry and the argot of the London streets, and invented words where none existing would suffice; a language, in short, appropriate to the range of the dramatic action, modulating from verse to prose and back to verse again. French writers, faithful to their tenets, pursued the ideal of decorum. Their characters were not drawn from common stock; they did not perform common actions; it was therefore inappropriate that they should use common language. We have seen how French tragic acting clung to the concept of the 'special voice', a kind of sing-song recitative that placed more emphasis on metrics than on sense, and gave the play an incantatory quality removing it from the world of common experience. In the same way the writers developed a 'special language' which avoided vulgar usage, working only in words and phrases fit for the noble ear. Thus, in describing the emotions, courtly euphemisms regularly occur. Though the passion of love is one of French tragedy's obsessions, its characters are rarely simply 'in love'. This is too blunt a statement of a brutal fact. They languish; they expire; they are consumed with flames.

But usually the effect is of extreme simplicity, even of sparseness. One statistic has become famous: Racine's dramatic vocabulary of 2000 words, as opposed to the 24,000 of Shakespeare. Yet here again simplicity can be a virtue. When simple words are used for rich emotions, the words become supercharged. One critic has compared Racine's verse to a kind of dramatic shorthand. The simple words are used as symbols, loaded with a whole context of associated meanings that must be filled out by the audience from its own emotional experience.

Yet the dramatist's asset has become the translator's liability, contributing to the lack of understanding of French tragedy in other cultures. The more florid the language is, the easier it is to translate. With the Dumas, Victor Hugo or Rostand we have had little trouble. But there is nothing harder to translate than perfect simplicity.

5 Racine: *Britannicus* and *Phèdre*

From the general considerations that governed the writing of French tragedy we may now turn to two particular examples. Both are by Jean Racine, an author whose works have survived in the living theatre when most of his contemporaries and rivals, even in France, have been forgotten or allowed to languish in academic obscurity. *Britannicus* deserves attention, first, because in Racine's preface to his published text he declared it as his own favourite; second, because the play's theme – the use and misuse of power in high places – has been seen as particularly applicable to our time, and has earned this work a number of recent revivals in several languages. The selection of *Phèdre* should need no explanation. Audiences and critics (at least after the original audience, which had some doubts) have universally declared it a masterpiece, the highest achievement of tragedy in its own time, and worthy to be ranked with the greatest plays of any age or country. What *Oedipus the King* is for the Greek theatre, or *Hamlet* for the Elizabethan, *Phèdre* has become for the French.

A word first about the author. Born in 1639, he lost both parents at an early age, and was brought up by his grandmother in the convent school of Port-Royal des Champs, outside Paris, where his family had connections; his aunt Agnès eventually became abbess there. Racine was thus introduced while still a boy to an institution which became famous in French ecclesiastical controversy, and with which he was to be involved, in one way or another, for the rest of his life. He broke from it, quarrelled with it, and was eventually reconciled with it; but its teachings left their mark, and helped to shape his plays.

Port-Royal was the centre of Jansenism, which had begun as a reform movement within the French Catholic Church. Named after its founder, Cornelius Jansen, Bishop of Ypres, the movement opposed itself to the formal piety which then seemed to dominate French religion. It taught a modified form of predestination, arguing that salvation could only come to the individual through the direct bestowal of God's grace. No man could justify himself merely by faith, church-going or good works. Love of God was the gift of God, to be given only at His pleasure. In a church already divided between Gallican and Ultramontane, between those who saw the King as the head of French Catholicism and those who looked over the Alps to Rome, a doctrine which departed so markedly from contemporary practices was bound to be severely scrutinised, and to create sensitivity both in its adherents and in its opponents. Rome kept up a running fire of criticism and condemnation. Port-Royal held out to the end. In 1710 its buildings were razed to the ground and its nuns distributed among other convents. In its time, however, it served not merely as a home for religious unorthodoxy but as a literary centre which produced Pascal as well as Racine, and a place of educational experiment.

Drawn early into the world of the theatre, Racine found himself harassed by Jansenist-inspired attacks on his chosen métier. Being thus embroiled, whether he liked it or not, in the running war between the French church and the French stage, he retorted testily but wittily upon his former mentors:

But we know how strict is your sense of moral propriety. We find it in no way strange that you condemn the poets. What does surprise us is your desire to stop mankind from paying them honour. Oh, my dear sir, be satisfied with putting the next world in order. Do not try to control the rewards of this one. You took your leave of it a long while ago. Let the world be judge of the things of this world. Accuse it, if you like, of being in love with trifles, and honouring those who create them. But do not envy such people the miserable honours which you have renounced for yourselves.

In writing such stuff, Racine was doubtless following fashion. It was politic at the time to criticise Port-Royal. Throughout his career Racine always had a shrewd eye for his own advantage. His first Paris play was produced by Molière's company. His second was snatched from them and given by him to the Hôtel de Bourgogne, the 'orthodox' house, whose established style offered a greater chance of commercial success. In his personal relationships Racine seems not to have been a pleasant man. But the competitive spirit of the French theatre did not encourage generosity. Wit, talent and a thick skin were needed to survive. Here is the tail-end of a sonnet that Racine composed about a rival's tragedy on the Trojan War:

From that point on, confusion ruled the play
More even than in Troy, that fatal day
When chaos struck, and all its men were slain.
Baron, on stage, could offer no reprieve.
The playwright's friends applauded, but in vain.
We yawned, or went to sleep, or took our leave.

A man who could write such things was not likely to make friends easily. But he was well able to look after himself.

Britannicus was first performed at the Hôtel de Bourgogne on 13 December 1669, with Floridor, the star of the company, in the role of the Emperor Nero – a fact which should tell us where the focus of the play was expected to be. In choosing Nero as a subject Racine had found a play which was virtually guaranteed to be popular; the twisted, enigmatic personality of this ruler has continued to excite the imaginations of writers and audiences through the centuries. There had been plays about Nero before Racine's. The earliest, a Latin tragedy called Octavia, may even have been written while Nero was still alive. It was attributed to Seneca, who functioned as Nero's tutor, advisor, minister and ghost-writer, and is customarily printed with that author's other tragedies drawn from more orthodox mythological subjects. Seneca himself appears as a character in the play. If he did write Octavia, however, he must have kept it firmly locked in his desk drawer, for the portrait it gives of Nero is a far from flattering one.

For obvious reasons, it was the monstrous Nero of popular legend that had the greatest appeal for playwrights. They could make dramatic capital out of his lurid crimes. There had already been French plays on the subject, the most successful being Tristan l'Hermite's La Mort de Senèque already mentioned. Racine took a different tack. His play shows not the villain already formed but the villain about to be. It focuses on the moment of choice that determines a career for good or ill, and illustrates the factors that cause that choice to be made.

Racine knew his Roman history well. He had read Tacitus, who leaves a detailed, if prejudiced, account of the early Empire, and adapts from him liberally. Although a knowledge of the historical situation is not strictly necessary to the understanding of the play – it stands on its own feet, and provides the audience with all the necessary information – it is interesting to compare the tragedy with its sources, and see what Racine chose to use or not to use, where he compressed, where he expanded and where he let his imagination run free. The historical situation was briefly this. In A.D. 54 the Emperor Claudius died. He was a man who had been conspicuously unhappy in his wives. The first, the notorious Messalina, had been executed for flagrant infidelity and suspicion of conspiracy against the throne. Various factions within the imperial household put forward candidates for her replacement, and Claudius' choice eventually fell upon Agrippina. He was undeterred by the fact that she was his own niece; emperors were above the charge of incest. Claudius already had a son by his previous marriage, Britannicus, so named in honour of the Emperor's campaigns in his newest province, and this boy should logically have succeeded to the throne. But Agrippina brought to the marriage a son of her previous union, Nero, whom she managed to insinuate into a position of precedence. Nero was soon established as a popular favourite, until it was a foregone conclusion that he and not Britannicus would succeed. Then Claudius died. There were rumours of unnatural death; it was believed that Agrippina had her husband poisoned as part of her grand design to give her son the Empire. Nero was promptly acclaimed as Emperor over Britannicus' head, leaving the young prince as a potential rival and, at the least, a dynastic embarrassment.

Nevertheless, Roman historians agree that the new Emperor made a good beginning. Racine was clearly intrigued by the falling off from this auspicious opening into the crimes, hatred and suspicion which marred the later years of the reign. He must have been seized by the passage in which Tacitus, though violently prejudiced against Nero, describes his first official speeches:

When he had gone through the form of mourning, he made his entrance into the Senate House and addressed its members, citing their authority and the will of the army. He quoted the precepts he had been given, and the examples available to him to follow whereby he could conduct his administration with conspicuous success. His youth, he pointed out, had not been spent in civil war, or marred by domestic strife. He harboured no grudges, meditated no reprisals, had no old scores to settle. He went on to outline his plans for the new regime, carefully disassociating himself from practices which had given offence in the recent past. He would not set himself up as the sole arbiter of the law, for when the whole machinery of justice was concentrated within the same four walls, a handful of people acquired influence out of all proportion to their numbers.

There would be no graft in his personal household, and no abuse of political patronage. His private life and official position would be kept firmly apart. The Senate would retain its time-honoured function. Cases involving Italy and the provinces governed directly by the Senate would be heard before the consular tribunal.

Tacitus is not alone in finding these sentiments deserving of applause. Other historians talk of the *quinquennium Neronis*, the first five happy years of Nero's reign. But how did he decline into the tyrant? This is the question that Racine investigates, and he selects as the decisive moment of Nero's fall from grace his murder of his rival Britannicus.

For dramatic clarity, Racine somewhat rearranges the personnel of history. One of the prime functions of drama, and particularly of this kind of drama, is to simplify. Tacitus' history is full of names. In the fierce rivalry of palace politics there were many who sought to bring their influence to bear on the new ruler. Racine selects a prominent few, in some cases changing history to do so. We see, of course, Nero himself. We see his mother Agrippina, who has brought her son to power and is fearful of seeing her influence diminish. In Tacitus, Nero has two advisors. One is Seneca, his tutor from an early age; the second is Burrhus, Captain of the Praetorian Guard, the 'kingmakers' whose military support was essential to any claimant to the throne. In Tacitus their roles are intricately intertwined, and they have their own interests to serve. Racine retains Burrhus, but Seneca is discarded as a character, being only briefly referred to in the play. To replace him Racine introduces Narcissus (Narcisse), a figure from slightly earlier imperial history; and he gives Narcissus and Burrhus more distinctly opposed personalities. Both serve as Nero's confidants (thus complicating the usual one-to-one relationship) but where Burrhus preaches moral uprightness and devotion to duty, Narcissus is always ready to pander to the baser side of Nero's nature, and to find ways for him to accomplish his secret desires. Thus, though the medieval drama is dead, we are presented with a triadic relationship of medieval symmetry, with Nero poised between his good and bad angels, listening to each in turn, and ultimately responding to the latter. The same two men serve as confidants to Britannicus, again duplicating and complicating the more usual principal-confidant relationship. Burrhus is honestly concerned with aiding Britannicus within the limits of his duty, while Narcissus gives him false advice and lures him to his destruction. Agrippina, we may note, has her own confidante in Albina (Albine) who plays a more conventional role in acting as feed and sounding-board to her mistress; she also functions as the Greek messenger in recounting the offstage events which bring the play to its conclusion.

The play is called *Britannicus*; the central event is the death of
Britannicus; but Britannicus is not the centre of the play. By Aristotelian standards he lacks the vital constituent of the tragic hero, the
propensity to error which leads his life astray (by which, one may
surmise, Aristotle meant simply that the wholly virtuous hero lacks
dramatic interest). He is the victim, snared and brought to his destruction by forces he cannot control or even comprehend. Britannicus goes
meekly to the slaughter. He commands our pity, but it is Nero who
commands our interest. Britannicus precipitates the dramatic situation.
He is the catalyst who induces action in others; and the play is named
for him in much the same way as *Julius Caesar* is named for a character
who is central to the action only in the sense that his death precipitates
a crisis. Finally, we have Junia (Junie), the girl with whom Britannicus
is in love. In spite of Racine's attempt, in a rather fussy and pedantic
preface, to identify her with a known figure of Roman history, she is
for all practical purposes an invented character. Like Britannicus, she is
a catalyst. Her beauty provokes Nero's lust, and his desire to secure her
gives him a further motive to destroy Britannicus.

We thus have a cast of only seven characters but with the potential
of highly complex relationships developing among them. We also have
a simple setting, which as usual can develop complex associations. 'La
scène est à Rome, dans une chambre du palais de Néron.' This is all that
the text specifies. But in this play, perhaps more than any other, the
simple room develops its sinister, claustrophobic potentialities. The vast
bulk of the palace, unseen offstage, slowly assumes the character of a
labyrinth. Racine drops hints of winding corridors, of tortuous passages,
of secret entrances. At the beginning of the play Agrippina (we may
continue, for simplicity, to use the classical versions of the names)
stands rooted by her son's door. She has kept an all-night vigil to be
sure of seeing him. But Nero eludes her; he has slipped out by another,
secret way.

The palace swallows up its victims. All passages seem to debouch
into this central room, where characters are led against their will to be
observed or tormented. There are spyholes through which Nero, the
spider who has built this web, may watch his victims. Here is Nero
describing the forced arrival of Junia at court:

> Last night I watched her come within this place,
> Distraught, and casting tear-filled eyes to heaven
> That sparkled from the glint of fire on armour,
> In beauty unadorned, the simple dress

Of loveliness snatched rudely from its sleep.
And then . . . I know not if her disarray,
Her savage captors with their brutal faces,
Her fear, gave greater lustre to her eyes.
It may be. Ravished by so fair a sight
I tried to speak to her, but stood dumbfounded,
Transfixed; my feet had lost the power to move.
I let her pass. She went to her own chamber
And I to mine, in which I sat alone
Trying – vain hope! – to wipe her face from mind.

Later, repulsed by Junia, the Emperor forces her to meet Britannicus
and tell him that she must renounce his love. He warns her that everything she says will be overheard:

I shall be hidden near, where I can watch you.
Bury your love within your deepest heart.
There is no word I cannot overhear,
No glance so subtle that I cannot read it.
Be sure of this. The smallest sigh of love,
The slightest touch, will seal his instant death.

Having trapped the lovers, Nero holds them in the room to torment
them. Once Britannicus is trapped within this web, he is doomed, and
the open door which eventually leads him from this room to what he
hopes will be a brighter world outside in fact leads only to his death.

Nero, not Britannicus, is the centre of this drama. But he is a weak
centre. We see him trying to cast off the forces which have shaped him,
and to assert his independence; but in shedding one influence, he merely
leaves himself open to another. A succession of forces play upon him,
tugging him this way and that. The first is his mother. Agrippina opens
the play, already fearful that her influence is waning, demeaning her
majesty by waiting like a petitioner at her son's door. Her concern is
less for Nero's character than for her own power:

Have I placed in his hands the reins of state
To let him govern at the Senate's will?
Let him be, if he so wills, his country's father,
But let him not forget he has a mother.

Again, Agrippina to Burrhus:

And have I elevated you so high
To interpose between my son and me?
Dare you not leave him to himself one moment?
Do you and Seneca contest the honour
Of separating Nero from his mother?
Have I entrusted him to you to make
Him thankless, and you rulers in his name?
The more I think, less credible it seems
That you could dare to count me as your creature,
You, whom I could have left to rot unknown,
Unrecognized, as captain of some legion,
And I, an empress, born of royal line,
Wife, daughter, sister, mother of your masters?

Burrhus answers as a blunt, honest soldier who has conscientiously performed the task assigned to him; who is aware, moreover, that the Emperor must be responsible to no man, and no woman:

You have entrusted Caesar's youth to me.
This I admit, and must remember ever.
But did I ever promise to betray him
And make him Emperor in name alone?
Who cares if Caesar listens to us still
Once we have shown him how a king should reign,
As long as he goes on in majesty
To keep Rome free, and Caesar's power unshaken?
Nero is sufficient to himself.
I follow. I do not presume to guide him.
For models, let him seek his ancestors.
With them for guide, his own success is sure.

Burrhus' protestations are soon to be proved false. Nero is not sufficient to himself. In casting off Agrippina, he has merely left himself open to a more pernicious influence. Agrippina, desperate for self-assurance, throws herself on the side of Britannicus, an act which helps to ensure the young prince's destruction; and Britannicus himself, entering the palace in search of his abducted Junia, is waylaid by Narcissus, who now has Nero's ear.

Narcissus is the active spirit of evil in this play. He represents the whole intricate, corrupt world of palace politics; a time-server, a parasite, he changes sides adroitly, plotting, scheming, lying, throwing his weight where he can see most benefit to himself. Skilled in deception, he can lure the naïve Britannicus with delusive hopes and false promises, and cynically warn him against such persons as himself:

> Sir, trust your secrets to discreet ears only,
> And do not bare your heart before the world.

This scene brings us to the end of Act One. (The formal division of tragedy into five acts was another principle inherited from Roman critics.) Notice how minimal, so far, the physical action has been. The play has proceeded mostly by long speeches, by harangues. Characters state their positions, amplify them, and develop the basic opposition between the court factions. Notice also that the most significant action so far has been a non-action, an entrance that fails to happen. After all Agrippina's attempts to see Nero, she has still not seen him. He has left by a secret way, and when his door opens it is Burrhus, not Nero, who emerges. Thus Racine both builds up interest in his principal character by postponing his appearance (Molière uses a similar device in *Tartuffe*) and prepares us for his evasiveness, his reluctance to meet issues face to face.

Act Two brings us Nero. His first appearance is not unsympathetic. We are still seeing him through Burrhus' eyes, as a young ruler learning to be master of himself, and his passion for Junia, which he describes in the speech already quoted, is an understandable human weakness. But Narcissus seizes on this very weakness to place his master under an obligation to him; he tells him what he wants to hear. Nero is already married; no matter. Narcissus can cite illustrious precedent for divorce:

> Your ancestor Augustus yearned for Livia;
> Both left their former mates and joined in wedlock.
> This fortunate divorce gave you the Empire.
> Tiberius, Augustus' son by marriage,
> Dared to his face repudiate his daughter.

The flatterer who quotes precedent to extenuate a dubious line of conduct is a familiar figure in Racine. We shall meet Narcissus' counterpart, and almost the same speech, in *Phèdre*.

Urged on by Narcissus, Nero reveals his passion to Junia. She repulses him. The role of empress holds no charms for her; she asks only for a quiet life, away from the seats of power. Nero, furious, forces her to dismiss Britannicus while he secretly looks on. But even this cannot calm his resentment of his rival – a resentment reinforced when the lovers meet again and he catches them unawares. By the end of Act Three Nero is firmly in Narcissus' hands. He has moved out of his mother's orbit; he has renounced Burrhus; he is set to move – or rather, to be moved by Narcissus, who is now the puppet-master who controls the play.

So far all has been preparation. Act Four is the act of events. We see, first, the confrontation between Nero and his mother. It begins with a stage direction, one of the very few that the text provides, and so simple that those who merely read the play may overlook its significance. It is no more than this: *Agrippine (s' asseyant).* Agrippina sits down. But when one considers the scene on stage, and particularly when one sees it in the light of the acting traditions of Racine's own time, the momentousness of this apparently trivial action becomes apparent. It is a double breach of propriety. First, in terms of the characters and their relationship, it is an offence against court protocol. Agrippina, in a last defiant burst of energy, snatches the initiative, sits down in the Emperor's presence, and condescends to him:

> Nero, come here, and take your seat beside me.
> They tell me I must answer your suspicions.
> What crimes they smear me with, I do not know,
> But all I've done I now lay bare to you.

Her action shows clearly that she still clings to the belief she earlier expressed to Burrhus. Nero may be Emperor, but he is still her son. She insists on deference, and a mother's rights. This scene used to be played by the Comédie Française, rather unfortunately, almost as a comic routine, with Nero and his mother offering each other seats with exaggerated courtesy. A pity, because this loses the shock effect. Racine's fashionable audience, preoccupied with the minutiae of etiquette, would instantly have recognised Agrippina's effrontery.

Secondly, Agrippina's action is an offence against stage protocol. In French tragedy, as in Greek, characters only rarely, and in exceptional circumstances, decline from the vertical. Sitting is a mundane action, unsuited to the dignity of declamatory verse. Here the breach of the norm marks the scene as one worthy of special attention, just as Racine's occasional, deliberate departures from the accepted pattern of French tragic verse make these lines stand out in their context. Once again we see how even the simplest action, on a stage that has been almost stripped of action, stands out in a sharp relief.

Events take their predictable course. Although Nero feigns a reconciliation with Agrippina, his heart is hardened against her and all who stand between him and his desires. Britannicus' death is in effect sealed from this moment. It remains only for Narcissus to overcome his remaining formal and perfunctory scruples and provide the poison whereby the murder will be done. In a short concluding act, Britannicus goes unsuspecting to his doom, his off-stage death is reported by Albina, and the other characters stand aghast at the monster who has arisen in their midst. Narcissus himself dies in the general debacle, but his spirit survives; and Nero has finally established his independence, finally made himself a ruler in fact as well as name, by treachery and bloodshed. The last line of the play belongs to Burrhus. Looking into the vista of horrors that the future holds, the discarded mentor prays sadly and ineffectually 'I wish this crime could be his last.'

Though rooted in Roman history, Racine's play is clearly more than historical drama. Psychologically, it is an exploration of human frailty. Politically, it is a cautionary tale, obvious enough perhaps to be dangerous in a country governed by an absolute monarchy. We have seen how Molière could select Corneille's *Nicomède* to flatter the ideal of kingship. *Britannicus* shows the darker image of the same institution. Corneille, it has been said, shows men as they should be, while Racine shows them as they are. There is some evidence that Louis XIV was aware of the parallels that might be drawn between the Roman tyrant and the Sun King. Contemporary gossip alleged that Louis, mindful of the fact that Nero had been a famous amateur theatrical performer, gave up dancing in the court ballets after *Britannicus* appeared. One must remember, too, that the conditions of performance helped to remove the story from its historical time and place and give it a more universal applicability. The architecture of the stage setting, though ostensibly Roman, was in fact classical design liberally interpreted through contemporary French eyes. Nor did the costumes make any pretence at historical accuracy. Actresses wore modern dress, the height of contemporary fashion. Actors wore a curiously stylised 'classical' costume which was neither Greek nor Roman, but owed its origins to costumer's fantasy and stage tradition: a helmet decorated almost to absurdity with high, nodding plumes, a canvas breastplate, boots, a sword. These were the costumes of ballet rather than of historical drama, creating a self-complete and self-sustaining stage world from which the audience might just as easily derive allusions to the present as information about the past.

The impulse for *Phèdre*, though still classical, came not from history but from a legend which has continued to inspire artists and writers across the centuries; which has begotten not merely a number of plays but films, novels and ballets. From his own Greek reading Racine was acquainted with the first extant dramatic manifestation of this story, *Hippolytus*, a tragedy written by Euripides in 428 B.C. This work follows the author's familiar pattern of setting up two characters who are polar opposites and who, by coming together, destroy each other in collision. It is set in the reign of Theseus, Athens' legendary hero-king, who is himself a major character in the play though he does not appear till late. Hippolytus, Theseus' son by a former marriage, is a young man devoted to hunting and the outdoor life. His chosen deity is Artemis, the goddess of the chase; he has no time for Aphrodite, the goddess of love. Indignant at this slight, Aphrodite inspires Phaedra, Theseus' second wife, with an incestuous passion for her stepson. Tormented by a love she dare not reveal, Phaedra is wasting away, and is almost at the point of death. Urged on by the chorus, Phaedra's old nurse forces her to reveal her secret, and the Queen's unwilling confession is brought to Hippolytus' ears. Hearing it under oath of secrecy, he is shattered by the revelation. He spurns his father's wife in loathing and disgust, and this rejection drives her to suicide. She secures posthumous revenge by leaving a letter accusing Hippolytus of raping her, so that she had no recourse but to kill herself. Hippolytus' sense of honour leaves him no defence; he cannot bring himself to break his oath of secrecy, even when accused by his own father. Theseus invokes a curse upon his son, which appears in the form of a sea-monster sent by the King's divine patron Poseidon. As the play closes Hippolytus' ravaged, broken body is brought onto the stage, and Artemis, the goddess he has always cherished, reveals the enormity of Theseus' error.

Hippolytus is a passionate play, beautiful and moving, and is still among the most frequently performed of the Greek repertory. It has, however, one inbuilt difficulty which continues to perplex actors and directors. Euripides clearly conceived this work as one in which the dramatic interest would be divided equally between the two principal characters. Hippolytus loves too little, Phaedra too much, and the human characters are framed by rival divinities whose antagonism provides the mainspring for the plot.

Yet in performance this does not work out. The balance is not equal, and Phaedra steals the show. Our sympathy is much more likely to go to a woman devoured by passion against her will than to a youth who seems frigid, self-satisfied and inhumanly unresponsive to the needs of others. Even in the author's lifetime his public was beginning to refer to the play as *Phaedra*, rather than by its given title. Interpreters have often tried to explain the unnatural austerity of Hippolytus by suggesting that he is homosexual. But there is no real evidence for this in the play, and it is doubtful whether such a concept entered Euripides' mind. It is not unlikely, however, that the possibility perplexed Racine. The way in which he solved this dilemma and gave Hippolytus more compelling motivations for his actions will appear below.

From Euripides the story passed to Seneca, whose tragedy was un-equivocally called *Phaedra* from the beginning. For a writer who specialised in studies of abnormality, the character of Phaedra was immediately attractive. In the Roman version the plot-line remains substantially the same, with the addition of a gruesome scene in which the remnants of Hippolytus' body, fragmented from his encounter with the monster, are reassembled by Theseus and the chorus.

Racine, with both the Greek and the Latin versions before him, made a number of obvious and important changes. Some of these are purely mechanical, and follow naturally from the exclusion of the chorus. The role of the Nurse is expanded to allow her to function as Phaedra's confidante throughout the play; she becomes Oenone, a lady-in-waiting at the royal court. Hippolytus is also given a confidant, Theramenes, his tutor, counsellor and friend. Although this type of character has no precedent in Euripides' play, he is familiar enough in other Greek tragedies, and Racine would not have needed to look far for a model. Both Oenone and Theramenes, as we have shown in Chapter 4, perform a chorus function in acting as sounding-boards to their principals and illuminating their characters through comment and conversation. Both, however, have other important ways in which they serve the plot. Theramenes, as messenger, delivers the finest narrative speech in the play, the description of Hippolytus' death in Act Five. Oenone not merely inherits the curiosity and meddlesomeness of the Nurse, but, like Narcissus in *Britannicus*, manipulates her royal mistress by pandering to her baser desires; thus she far transcends the usual confidante role. Notice that by these changes and additions Racine has arrived at a disposition of characters very much in the pattern of his time, and more symmetrical even than in Euripides' split-focus play. We shall see more evidence of this symmetry shortly.

Another change involves the deities who open and close Euripides' play and are present by reference and allusion throughout. Racine wrote for an audience both Christian and rationalist, for whom the glorification of pagan goddesses would have had little interest or meaning. Artemis and Aphrodite no longer appear on stage. The apparatus of Greek mythology, however, cannot be removed entirely for it is too deeply interwoven into the fabric of the story. Phaedra still represents herself as the prey of Aphrodite, or rather, in her Roman incarnation, Venus. Theseus still prays to Neptune (Poseidon) to bring about the fatal curse. Phaedra still looks back to the gods among her ancestors. But most of these references, though pagan in language, can be shown to be Christian in thought. Instead of the arbitrary interference by anthropomorphic deities in human affairs, we are offered Jansenist predestination; the emphasis has shifted from the divine machinery to the human motivations of the characters and the way in which they exacerbate each other.

There is one other, more important, change, which again involves an added character. This is the Princess Aricia, last survivor of the house that challenged Theseus' domination of Athens, with whom Hippolytus has had the misfortune to fall in love. Racine justifies her inclusion by citing Virgil as well as Greek mythological sources. In fact she is, like Junia in *Britannicus*, a product of the author's mind, but far more important than Junia in her character and actions. The playwright's motive for introducing her is to make Hippolytus more culpable by being guilty of an error; Racine is, in fact, being faithful to Aristotelian theory, and Hippolytus becomes at once more human and more interesting. The young prince is in love with his father's enemy, a girl forbidden by law to marry for fear that she may propagate a rival dynasty. Aricia summarises her own plight:

> The last descendant of an earth-born king,
> I was the sole survivor of the war;
> Saw taken, in the flower of their youth,
> Six brothers, high hope of a noble house.
> The sword reaped harvest, and the sodden earth
> Swallowed the sad draught of my brothers' blood.
> And since their death, you know the stern decree
> Forbidding any man in Greece to love me.
> They feared one day the sister's reckless flames
> Might breathe new life into her brothers' ashes.

In loving her, Hippolytus defies his father's edict; and for an audience conscious of dynastic issues in its own society, talk of civil war and a divided state would have reawakened memories of recent history. But there is no doubt a secondary, though still powerful, reason for Aricia's existence. Through her Racine removes any suspicion of Hippolytus' homosexuality. In a society where homosexuality was a capital offence, and the King's brother a notorious homosexual, this was an issue to be avoided at all costs. Moreover, the existence of a rival gives Phaedra added incentive to destroy Hippolytus. As we shall see, Racine plays on female jealousy in a way that was not accessible to Euripides.

We thus have a play which is balanced with almost perfect mathematical symmetry. Both of the principal characters have illicit loves. Both have advisors whose function is to suggest, more or less honorably, what the ordinary person would do in such a predicament. But, as we have noted before, these are not ordinary people but royalty, and their individual desires should, ideally, bow before the obligations thrust upon them by their station. Thus their dilemma is no longer purely moral. The balance of interest has shifted. There are important social and political repercussions in any action they may take. Hippolytus is always aware of his disloyalty to his father's regime. Phaedra, even in the depths of her passion, is miserably conscious of how far she falls short of the monarchic ideal. And Theseus, for the same reason, assumes a larger role than in Euripides' play. He is the king. We may note that, in the cast-lists of this period, characters tend to be listed by social rank, rather than by dramatic importance; the king comes first. From him all decisions come, round him ultimately all things revolve; and *Phèdre*, no less than *Britannicus*, is a play about the decision-making process, and the dangers to which a supreme ruler is liable.

Theseus, though his appearance is deferred until Act Three, is thus a pivotal figure. His initial absence creates an unnatural lacuna at the centre of things, a state of unregulated confusion in which improper events may occur. His reappearance precipitates action and brings about a crisis; his decisions, though misguided, are irrevocable. Racine gives us a figure glittering with the lustre of his rank and the prestige that his exploits have acquired, but still possessing clear faults. For Euripides' audience Theseus was a national hero, the father-figure of Athens. Racine's character is invested with the same glory. He is still the slayer of monsters, the giant killer, the champion of civilisation against barbarism. So Hippolytus describes him to Theramenes:

> Bound to me by unfailing loyalty
> You used to tell me stories of my father.
> You know my heart hung on your every word
> And warmed to tales of his heroic deeds
> When you depicted that proud warrior
> Consoling mankind for the death of Hercules:

Slaughter of monsters, punishment of rovers,
Procrustes and Cercyon, Scyron, Sinnis,
Epidaurus littered with its giant's bones,
Crete reeking with the blood of Minotaur.

He continues in the same vein to Theseus' face in Act Three:

Even before you had attained my years
More than one tyrant, more than one wild beast
Had felt the heavy summons of your arm.
You were already the oppressor's scourge,
Protector of the peoples of two seas;
Men travelled free, and plied their trade in peace;
Hercules heard the fame of your achievements
And rested easy, leaving you his load.

But Theseus had less admirable traits, uncomfortably reminiscent – as contemporary audiences must have suspected, and later critics have insisted – of Louis XIV himself. He had been a notorious womaniser, as Hippolytus recognises to his sorrow:

But when you told less admirable tales,
The easy vows pledged in a hundred places,
Helen of Sparta ravished from her parents,
Periboea weeping upon Salamis,
So many others, even their names forgotten,
Too trusting spirits cheated by his passion,
Ariadne weeping in the wilderness,
Then Phaedra, taken under better omens,
You know how sadly I listened to this story
And urged you often to pass over it,
Happy if I could only wipe from mind
This sordid chapter of so fair a tale . . .

Theramenes insists that the King has settled down in happy marriage, but the doubts persist. Aricia too recognises Theseus' fallibility; he is prone to hasty judgement, too ready to listen to the wrong people; he displays, in a word, all the glory and all the weakness of absolute monarchy.

Now to the play. The stage setting is, as we have already established, at least partially 'open', indicating both inside and outside the palace.

But there is still, from the beginning, a sense of unnatural confinement hardly less powerful than in *Britannicus*. The characters are rooted in this place, and though they would like to escape, cannot. They are bound by their desires or their obligations. The play's first lines, spoken by Hippolytus, express his desire to leave, to go adventuring in search of his father. But he does not go. Love for Aricia, the love he hardly dares admit to himself, restrains him. In Hippolytus' confession to Theramenes we have the nuclear dilemma of French tragedy, the flesh against the spirit, desire at war with sense of duty.

> But even if my proud heart could be softened
> Should I choose Aricia for my conqueror?
> Rather my errant thoughts should have remembered
> The eternal barrier that stands between us.
> My father holds her dangerous, and imposes
> Stern laws to block her brothers' line in her.
> He fears the tainted branch may bear green shoots
> And seeks to bury their name with their sister.
> She's bound his ward until the grave receives her.
> No torch will ever light her wedding day.
> Should I wed her cause, and flout my father's anger,
> Set myself up as a bold example,
> Launch my youth on the shifting shoals of love . . .

Theramenes' answer is the straightforward response of an honest man who sees no problem. It is, quite simply, 'Why not?'

> But come, why fear an honourable love
> And shrink to venture what has sweets to give?
> Will you always keep your chastity for guide?
> Many a manly heart's gone down to Venus!
> Where would you be yourself, you renegade,
> If Antiope had stood firm against her laws
> And never burned with maiden love for Theseus?
> Why talk as if you still despised such things?

His attempted suasion only emphasises Hippolytus' dilemma.

The play proceeds upon its balanced way. Following the revelation of Hippolytus' love we witness that of Phaedra's, in a scene of parallel construction, and just as we saw Hippolytus in relation to his father, we now see Phaedra in terms of her ancestors. For Racine's audience, heredity was important. Hippolytus is in many ways his father's son, and we are introduced to Phaedra as her mother's daughter, 'the daughter of Minos and Pasiphaë'. She comes from a line which has been conspicuously plagued by the weakness of the flesh. Pasiphaë lusted after a bull, and disguised herself as a cow to mate with him. From this monstrous union the bull-headed Minotaur was born. The inference is obvious: all of Minos' progeny are in some sense monstrous, as Phaedra recognises when she lists her family tree:

PHAEDRA Hatred of Venus, and her fatal anger!
         Oh mother, what dark ways you walked for love!
OENONE   Let us forget them, and in time to come
         Inter this memory in lasting silence.
PHAEDRA My sister Ariadne, racked by love,
         Abandoned on the shore and left to die!
OENONE   What are you doing? What torments your mind
         To make you cry against your family?
PHAEDRA Venus has spoken. Last of my sad line
         And the unhappiest, I too shall die.
OENONE   Are you in love?
PHAEDRA   In love? I am possessed!

Phaedra is presented as one predestined to sin, as one from whom divine grace has been withdrawn. Conscious of her guilt, she abhors her fatal passion and has tried every way to prevent it, but in vain. The Jansenist influence in her speech is obvious:

I felt my body turn to ice and fire,
Knew Venus and her all-devouring flame,
The torments destined for her chosen victims.
I thought to turn them off by tireless prayer,
Built her a temple, made it beautiful,
And hourly stood among the sacrifices
Hunting my lost wits in their gutted bodies.
Poor remedy for passion past all healing!
In vain my hands burnt incense at her altars.
My lips invoked the goddess, but my heart
Hippolytus. I saw him everywhere,
His image knelt beside me at the altar . . .
No more is it a subtle, secret passion
But Venus incarnate, battened on her prey.

Phaedra's declaration is immediately followed by the announcement of Theseus' death, and Oenone's initial horror turns to optimism. Like Theramenes, her response is now 'Why not?'

> Your fortune's changed, and wears a different face;
> The King is dead, and you must take his place! . . .
> Live! You've no cause now to accuse yourself.
> Your love's a lawful love, like any other.
> Theseus has severed by his death the ties
> That made your love a foul and guilty thing.
> Hippolytus holds little terror now,
> You'll not be guilty if you look at him.

The pragmatic view wins. Phaedra takes Oenone's advice, as Hippolytus took that of Theramenes, and the act concludes with two new declarations imminent.

Act Two, like Act One, is split into two balanced sections. The news of Theseus' death, which calmed Phaedra's conscience, has also left Hippolytus free to declare himself to Aricia. He offers her the kingdom, and his heart.

> I've gone too far.
> My passion has proved stronger than my reason.
> But madam, now that I have broken silence
> I must go on as I started, and reveal
> A secret that I can no longer keep.
> There stands before you an unhappy prince
> Whom headstrong pride has modelled in her image.
> I, who disdained to walk the ways of love
> And mocked her prisoners these many years,
> Who thought that I could stand safe on the shore
> For ever, and watch others fight the storm,
> How sadly do I see myself translated!

Although Aricia's acceptance of his love is interrupted by the arrival of the Queen, she leaves him with hope:

> Go, Prince, pursue your generous intent.
> Make Athens tributary to my power.
> All that you would give me, I accept.
> But you have given me a gift more precious
> Than all the might and majesty of empire.

Hippolytus' avowal of love is now matched by Phaedra's avowal to him, in one of the most turbulent and tormented scenes that French tragedy produced. Phaedra attempts to speak calmly. She is pleading, she says, for her son, not for herself. But gradually her passion overwhelms her, and social restraints are cast aside in a speech in which the sexual symbolism is blatant:

> Yes, Prince, I pine, I burn for Theseus' love.
> I love him – not the Theseus Hades saw,
> The fickle lover of a thousand conquests
> Who sought to sully Pluto's marriage bed,
> But faithful, proud ... perhaps a little shy,
> Youthful and handsome, winning every heart,
> Made in the likeness of the gods ... or yours.
> His face had that same tint of modesty,
> He had your bearing, had your eyes, your speech
> When he crossed the waters to our land of Crete,
> A fit man for the love of Minos' daughters!
> What were you doing then? When he assembled
> The flower of Greece, where was Hippolytus?
> Why were you still so young you could not sail
> On board the ship that carried him to shore?
> By your hand then the Minotaur had died
> Despite the windings of his vast retreat;
> To save you from perplexity my sister
> In your hands would have placed the fatal thread.
> But no; in this I would have been before her,
> Love would have given me first inspiration.
> I would have been your help, Prince, I your guide
> To learn the windings of the labyrinth.
> What care I would have lavished on your head,
> And sought more surety for love than thread!
> Companion in the danger you must seek
> I would have gone before you on your way
> And Phaedra would have plumbed the labyrinth
> With you, and we'd emerge or die together!

As in Euripides, Hippolytus is repelled by these ardent protestations. In despair, Phaedra snatches his sword and attempts to stab herself. We have already considered this incident as an example of Racine's restrained use of stage violence: a simple action which assumes enormous

consequence in a play which, up to this point, has been virtually actionless, and which, like Phaedra's preceding speech, has an obvious sexual
symbolism. Oenone drags Phaedra from the stage, leaving Hippolytus
aghast and barely able to comprehend what he has heard. The sword
remains in Phaedra's hands, to be used in false evidence against its
owner.

Act Three, the central, pivotal act, begins with Phaedra's grief at
what she has done, and Oenone's assumption of a more active role.
Another Narcissus, she seizes on the weakness of her mistress to offer
various courses of action. Hippolytus may be bribable; he may accept
Phaedra together with the throne. (Again dynastic issues thrust themselves on our attention.) But all is thrown into confusion by another
piece of news, a thunderbolt. Theseus is not dead. He lives, he has
returned. The need for action is immediate. Again it is Oenone who
takes the dominant role. Accuse Hippolytus, she tells her mistress,
before he accuses you. Frightened and emotionally exhausted, with no
will left of her own, Phaedra allows herself to be persuaded. Thus, when
Theseus makes his delayed appearance, the stage is set for a confrontation.

We may pause here to note one instance of Racine's rationalising
mind at work, even when his subject is taken from remote legend. In
the original sources, Theseus had indeed 'died' in the sense that he had
descended to the Underworld. Emulating the Labours of Hercules,
though for less honourable motives, he had gone down to Hades to
assist his friend Peirithous to kidnap Persephone, Queen of the Dead. The
plan went awry. Peirithous remained captive in the Underworld, while
Theseus was miraculously restored by Hercules' intervention. Racine,
who consistently suppresses the supernatural elements in his story,
provides an alternative explanation:

> Gods, why did you free me from imprisonment
> If fear and coldness wait for me at home?
> I had one friend; but he, with lust's effrontery
> Looked covetously upon Epirus' queen.
> Reluctantly I helped his amorous intent
> But angry destiny had blinded us.
> The king caught me unready, weaponless.
> I wept sad tears to watch Peirithous
> Flung by this savage to the cruel beasts
> That fed on his unhappy victims' blood.
> Me he kept captive in his caves, so dark

And deep they border on the realm of death.
Six months, and then the gods took note of me.
I found a way to cheat my jailer's eyes
And cleansed the world of this offence to nature.
His body served as browsing for his beasts.

And so the patterns of the play coalesce into a tableau. In the centre
Theseus, suspicious, stern in judgement, embodying all the might and
majesty of kingship. On one side, Phaedra, for the moment Oenone's
puppet, uttering half-comprehended accusations. On the other, Hippolytus, unable to defend himself without uncovering his stepmother's
shame, and conscious, too, of his own guilt in his father's eyes should
his intentions toward Aricia be discovered.

In Act Four the tableau fragments, sending the characters spinning
off again upon their diverse courses. As in *Britannicus*, this is the act
of decision, in which things are done that will have irrevocable consequences. The tempo increases. We have a series of short, bitter, passionate scenes. First comes the interview between Theseus and Oenone, in
which the confidante presses Phaedra's false charges, offering Hippolytus'
sword as evidence. Some concessions are made to the more delicate sense
of French propriety. It is no longer claimed, as in Euripides, that
Hippolytus has raped Phaedra, merely that he has attempted to. Racine
makes a major point of this in his preface; he wishes to purge the play
of grossness. But the lesser charge is still sufficient to awaken Theseus'
wrath. In the scene following he angrily accuses Hippolytus, who is
unable to speak a word in his own defence; he can only admit his true
fault, his love for Aricia. Theseus contemptuously dismisses this as a
pretence, and as Hippolytus leaves the stage the curse is spoken:

Unhappy boy, you go to certain death.
Beside the waters where the very gods
Walk trembling, Neptune pledged his word to me
And he will keep it. In your shadow treads
An ever-present and avenging god.
I loved you once; in spite of your offence
My heart already weeps for what must be,
But you have left no way but to condemn you.
Did ever father suffer greater wrong?
Just gods, who look upon my load of sorrow,
How could I have begotten such a son?

The curse, as we have noted, is one element of the supernatural that Racine cannot rationalise. It is too deeply embedded in the plot. The curse must be spoken, and it must work. But we may, without undue strain, see it as a metaphor; the power of the curse stands for the awesome power of the monarch, who may shatter lives with a single word.

Enter Phaedra, alarmed by the commotion, apprehensive of what she might have brought about. Although she dares not reveal the truth, she tries to soften the father's anger against the son. And then Racine's master stroke of psychology, a contribution that is all his own and owes nothing to Euripides: Theseus, in letting slip the fact that Hippolytus claims to love Aricia, awakens Phaedra's instant jealousy, and all thoughts of repentance vanish from her mind.

> Oh, he can love; but he can not love me!
> Aricia has his heart! Aricia!
> Gods! When he cased his cold ingratitude
> In eye so scornful and in brow so stern
> I thought his heart was ever shut to love
> And barred to every woman as to me.
> But another woman bent his stubborn spirit!
> Another woman taught his eyes to smile!
> Perhaps his heart is anybody's prize,
> Accessible to everyone but me,
> And I would take it on me to defend him!

Her desolation is complete. She sees herself as irrevocably damned, in a speech again filled with mythological allusion but capable of interpretation in a Christian context:

> What right have I to live, to look upon
> The pure bright sun, the founder of my race?
> I claim the king and father of the gods
> For my progenitor; throughout the universe,
> Throughout wide heaven are my ancestors.
> Where can I hide? In the dark underworld?
> No, there's my father, in his ruthless hands
> The urn of judgement given him by Fate,
> Minos, before whose court pale men must come.
> How his ghost will cry out in astonishment
> To see his daughter present in his sight,
> Compelled to read the roster of her crimes,

So new, so strange, unheard of even in Hell.
What will you say, my father, when you see me?
I can imagine how the dreadful urn
Will tumble from your hands; I can imagine
How you will cast about for some new punishment,
To be your own child's executioner.
Forgive! A cruel god has crushed your house.
Behold his vengeance in your daughter's frenzy
I'm driven by the shame of my offence
That never tasted any of its joys.

Oenone, as usual, can find justification and a precedent for sinning:

My lady, there is nothing here to fear.
Look with new eyes. This is no mortal sin.
You fell in love. We cannot fight our fate.
You were bewitched and not accountable.
Is this so strange and wonderful a thing?
Are you the only woman in the world
Whom love has won? To err is only human.
You are mortal, so accept your mortal lot.
The very gods, the gods of high Olympus
Who thunder terror into sinners' ears
Have known the stirrings of illicit love.

But this kind of counsel can be of no help to Phaedra now. She is too far gone; and now, when it is too late, she sees Oenone clearly for what she is:

I'll hear no more from you. I hate you. Go.
Leave me to bear my burden by myself.
May heaven pay you in your own bad coin,
And may your punishment be an example
To all who pander to the weaknesses of princes
By fawning artifice, and smooth their path to crime—
Vile flatterers, the most pernicious gift
That angry heaven could have made to kings.

There must have been several among Racine's courtly audience who winced at that concluding statement.

In Act Five the curse comes to fulfilment. Aricia, having parted sadly from Hippolytus as he goes to exile, attempts to bring his father to a knowledge of the truth. She reminds him that even kings may err, that the giant-killer has been cherishing an undetected foe:

> Take care, my lord, take care. Unsmiling heaven
> May hate you well enough to bring your curse
> To pass; for often in its anger it will take
> The victims that we offer. Heaven's gifts
> Are often punishments to fit our crimes . . .
> Have a care, my lord. Your all-conquering hand
> Delivered men from monsters without number.
> But all are not destroyed. You have left one
> Alive . . .

Theseus wavers; he begins to feel that he may have committed a misjudgement. But it is now too late for repentance. Just as his resolution shifts, Theramenes appears to deliver the messenger speech. In Racine's version, we do not see Hippolytus' mangled body. He is not carried in, as in Euripides, to breathe his last on stage. But Theramenes' narrative is so vivid that we may imagine we have watched him at the moment of death. The speech is a masterpiece of dramatic narrative. Morbid, powerful, self-contained, it has remained a favourite test-piece for French actors to the present day.

> We had that minute passed the gates of Troezen.
> He rode his chariot; his dejected men
> Borrowed his silence and surrounded him.
> Sadly he followed the Mycenae road,
> Letting the reins hang on his horses' backs.
> His noble steeds, who formerly were seen
> High-stepping to his call, and mettlesome,
> Now paced with drooping head and downcast eye
> As sympathetic to his melancholy.
> Then from the water's depths a fearful cry
> Came shattering the stillness of the air . . .
> The wave came in, broke, and before our eyes
> Threw up a raging monster in the surf,
> His huge head barbed and menacing with horns,
> A yellowed plaque of scales upon his body,
> A man-devouring bull, a fiery dragon.

Only Hippolytus had courage to attack the monster, but his horses bolted in fear:

> They were panic-stricken, and for once struck deaf
> Ran heedless of their master's hand and voice.
> He spent his strength to hold them, but in vain.
> Their mouths frothed blood until the bit was red . . .
> The axle shrieked and snapped; Hippolytus
> Saw his chariot go down in splinters. . . .
> His blood lay spotted on the road to guide us;
> The rocks were red with it, the ugly thorns
> Were hung with scarlet drops and matted hair.
> I came and called him. He stretched out his hand,
> His eyes half opened, and then closed again.
> 'Heaven' he said 'has taken my blameless life.
> Comfort Aricia when I am gone.
> Friend, if the scales fall from my father's eyes
> And he mourns the sad death of his slandered son,
> To appease my death and my unhappy ghost
> Tell him to treat his prisoner with kindness
> And give her back . . .' On this the Prince fell dead.
> My arms held nothing but his broken bones,
> Sad trophy of the anger of the gods.
> Even a father's eyes would not have known him.

Hippolytus is not the only one to die. Oenone, we learn, has drowned herself; Phaedra, confronting Theseus for the final time, has already taken poison. Her first words in the play were a cry for the sun, and her last are a farewell to the light of day. Theseus is left to pick up the fragments of his shattered life. There is hope, at the end, that the King may have learnt from his mistakes. His enmity with Aricia is at an end. Obedient to Hippolytus' dying wish, he will adopt her as his daughter.

Phaedra herself remains one of the most fascinating and complex characters of this kind of drama, or indeed of any drama. Different actresses have seen her in different ways. Her two most famous contemporary French interpreters have revealed widely divergent concepts of the part. Edwige Feuillère played Phaedra from the beginning as a victim, incapable of resisting the forces acting upon her though she recognised their power and their evil. Marie Bell, on the contrary, emphasised the monstrous aspect of the character. Her Phaedra had purple hair, and long gold talons for fingernails; she was a demon incarnate, come to destroy. Yet the fascination of Phaedra lies in the fact that she embraces both of these characters, and is above all transcendently human. Phaedra is a woman's role created by a theatre which had, after centuries, at last admitted women to full membership; and her most outstanding characteristic is perhaps her femininity.

This was the last play that Racine wrote for the commercial theatre. The reasons for his retirement remain unclear. It has been speculated that his candid treatment of the monarchy struck too close to home, and that he was, in effect, warned off. Alternatively, it has been suggested that the initial reception of *Phèdre* estranged him from the theatre. His play was received comparatively coldly, while his rival Pradon's tragedy on the same subject was judged a success. There is some evidence that his opponents formed a clique against him to dampen the enthusiasm of the audience at the *première*, though stories of the packing of the theatre by his rivals seem to be exaggerated. Or perhaps Racine was simply tired. In the closing years of his career, the intervals between his plays grew noticeably longer; he may well have felt that he had written himself out, and welcomed a retreat from the competitive world of the theatre to more leisurely and contemplative composition.

The judgement of the first audience was speedily reversed. *Phèdre* survives, and will continue to be played, despite all the difficulties inherent in recreating Racine's world for a modern, and particularly for a non-French speaking, audience. These difficulties are real, and perhaps ultimately insuperable, for the qualities instinctive to Racine's craft are precisely those which jar upon modern theatrical sensibilities. In the foregoing account of *Phèdre*, much has been made of the symmetry and balance of the play. In Racine's time this was not merely desirable but virtually mandatory. A society cultivating the classical virtues prided itself or its sense of logic, order and reason, and balance and harmony were a necessary manifestation of these qualities in the arts. We hear this is baroque music; we see it in contemporary architecture; we observe it even in the taming of nature to conform to aesthetic principles. The symmetry of *Phèdre* is the symmetry of Versailles, where fountain responds to fountain, where trees match trees in orderly and measured rows, just as speech matches speech and scene balances scene in the play. Modern audiences find the language and structure of the play too formal for the passions it contains; they may claim that it is unnatural, artificial. Yet Racine certainly thought that he was reproducing nature, albeit nature ordered by a controlling hand. He was writing of the passion of love for a society where love was an ornate ritual to be approached with proper ceremony, not a brute fact; the lengthy and elaborate declarations of ardour in Racine have been compared to the complex mating-dances of bees. This formality cannot be forfeited without grave loss to the play. Certainly the formal, almost stilted language is at odds with the passions expressed, but this is part of the point. Racine's plays belong to the drama of the baroque; and one school of thought derives that much-disputed word from the Portuguese *barroco,* a pearl that is not a perfect sphere, as though some inner pressure had warped it out of true. Whether or not this derivation is accurate, it is apt for our dramatic purpose. The form of the play strains to confine its content; and from the tension between the two arises the drama.

6 Dances and Machines

In considering the development of French tragedy, and the extent to which it was influenced by classical models, we noted one conspicuous absence. In French drama, there is no real equivalent of the chorus whose songs and dances were once the heart, and always the characteristic feature, of classical Greek tragedy and comedy. We suggested, as one reason for this, the economic necessities of the professional theatre. Mass spectacle of such a nature could survive only while drama was still a community art produced by amateurs for their peers. We suggested also, however, that the Greek chorus did have an approximate equivalent in the one area of French entertainment where it was still economically feasible. This was the rarefied world of the court ballet.

For interpretive dance of this nature, French critics could find classical precedents almost as easily as they had been able to find models for tragedy. In the Greek and Roman theatre, when dance had disappeared from the drama proper, it had survived as an independent art form, though practised by solo interpreters rather than by groups. The later classical *pantomimus* specialised in presenting the familiar stories of myth and legend in terms of movement alone. Dancing to the music of a flute, or simple percussion instruments, he enacted the adventures of Oedipus and Iphigeneia, of Atreus and Thyestes; and there were critics of note who professed to find these renditions aesthetically superior to the tragedies which had arisen from the same sources. In the later, debased days of the ancient theatre, when tragedy had become stilted, declamatory and pompous and could no longer appeal to a popular audience, the dancer was seen as a purer and more sympathetic artist, whose performance could transcend the limitations of language and make a vivid and immediate appeal to the spectator's emotions. Parallels were drawn between the literary and visual arts, showing that one could serve as the equivalent of the other. Horace, in his *Ars Poetica*, made the analogy between poetry and painting (*ut pictura poesis*). Plutarch, writing in Greek in the first century A.D., argued that poetry was a 'talking picture'; and on this basis dance could be justified on pure aesthetic grounds as a moving picture, poetry in motion. In the second century A.D. Lucian wrote a monograph *On Dance* in which he compared pantomime and tragedy, greatly to the discredit of the latter. Though primarily a satirist, Lucian was not on this occasion writing with tongue in cheek. He argued that dance could portray all the favourite themes and characters of tragedy without the absurdities incidental to the conventional dramatic performance, and appended a long list of subjects to which the dancer might profitably turn his attention.

Dance, then, was seen as tragedy purged of the superfluity of language. By illustrative and symbolic gesture it could not merely relate the story but communicate its wider ramifications. Being by nature a more abstract art than tragedy, dance could more easily remove the fable from its immediate place and time and give it a more universal application. All arts, said Plutarch, are an imitation, in that they seek to copy the world at large. They differ only in the means of their realisation, and the dancer can operate on an allegorical level not easily accessible to the dramatic actor.

French critics, theorising about the performing arts, found this notion of dance as an abstract art appealing. Menestrier, who composed a formidable treatise entitled *Ancient and Modern Ballets According to the Rules of the Theatre*, described ballet as the elder brother of music, painting and poetry, combining the most important features of all of them. He also evolved a definition typical of its place and time. In the theatres, he argued, comedy imitates the actions of the people, and tragedy those of the nobility, while ballet can do both these things and more; it penetrates to the very essence of things, so that intellectual concepts can be presented just as easily as flesh-and-blood characters. In a theatre preoccupied with dramatic genres and the kinds of subject-matter appropriate to each, ballet offered the opportunity of presenting complex forms not available to the drama of the spoken word.

Although dance was the essence of French ballet, however, the sung or spoken word was still present. This combination could be supported not merely by reference to the original Greek chorus, but by the inherent musicality of French dramatic verse. As we have seen, the lines in French tragedy were not simply spoken, but chanted in a kind of recitative. French critics saw this as an approximation to the dramatic delivery of the ancients (as it probably was) and there were a number of attempts in the sixteenth century to recreate the musical notations of Greek verse. Thus we shall see the French court ballet, when it has evolved to its full glory, employing the talents not merely of dancing-masters but of librettists also; and the librettists are more often than not the major playwrights of the age.

Finally, for those who argued that the performing arts should have a higher end than mere entertainment, ballet could be justified on a metaphysical level as representing, in tangible and earthly form, the divine harmony of the universe, the music of the spheres. In his *Epithalamium for the Marriage of Prince Henri of Lorraine and Catherine of Cleves*, performed in Paris in 1570, Jean Dorat appropriately expresses this idea in song. There are two choruses, who responsively proclaim the concept of social harmony as embodied in the dance:

> The world from discord comes to full accordance.
> The King fears God; the Princes bow before
> The King, and give to lesser men the law.
> So let us dance, to have no more discordance.
> Each one in turn must bow before the other
> From smallest to the greatest of the great,
> Maintaining rank and orderly estate,
> So all may dance in harmony together.

The same idea, only slightly exaggerated for comic effect, is expressed by Molière a century later in *Le Bourgeois Gentilhomme*, in a scene where the Music Master and Dancing Master attempt to convince their patron of the importance of their arts:

MM Philosophy's all very well in its way. But music, sir, music . . .

MD Music and dance. Music and dance give you all you need.

MM Music is the lifeblood of the nation.

DM The dance is food and drink to me.

MM Without music, it's impossible for the country to survive.

DM Without dance, we're back in the dark ages.

MM All the wars and disasters of history only happened because people didn't know music.

DM All human misfortunes, all the great calamities of ages past, all the blunders of politicians, all the military defeats, have come about because people didn't know how to dance.

M. JOURDAIN What are you talking about?

MM What is war? A lack of communion among men!

M.J. That's true.

MM   And if all men learned music, would they not find a means of
         achieving harmony, and see an age of universal peace?

M.J. You're right.

DM   When a man has made some misjudgement in his family affairs,
         or in matters of state, or in military strategy, don't we
         always say 'So and so has made a false step in such and
         such?'

M.J. Yes, that's what we always say.

DM   And why do we make a false step? Because we don't know how
         to dance! That is the sole reason!

It was natural, therefore, for ballet to develop a high moral tone, to
evolve as a kind of theatrical allegory and, given the nature of its
audience, to draw heavily on classical plots and characters. There was
material in abundance. Later writers, following Lucian's example, ran-
sacked classical mythology for suitable stories. These eventually
became available in handy manuals like Giraldi's *Genealogy of the
Gods,* or Ripo's *Iconology.* Many of these themes and characters were,
in any case, already familiar to audiences through existing aspects of
court ceremonial, on which the emergent ballet could build. The proces-
sional entry of a monarch into any European city was regularly marked
by tableaux, playlets and addresses of welcome spoken by performers
garbed as ancient deities, allegorical figures or the classical virtues.
Such incidents could easily be embodied as units in a connected ballet.
Another form of allegorical spectacle with which noble audiences were
well acquainted was the tournament, which continued to flourish as an
entertainment long after the practical need for its existence had
vanished. Tournaments had come into being as the war games of the
early Middle Ages. By testing horsemanship and other knightly skills
in a competitive setting, they trained the participants to prepare for
war; the *seigneur* who jousted with a friendly rival in the lists one day
might have to charge an enemy in deadly earnest on the next. With the
invention of gunpowder the armoured knight was rendered obsolete;
but the tournament, a popular spectator sport, lingered on for years,
becoming more fanciful and decorative as its utility declined. It had
long been customary to arouse excitement and interest by giving the
tournament a rudimentary plot. A scenic fortress was erected in the
centre of the arena. On this stood a selection of the ladies of the court,
often dressed as characters from classical legend or medieval romance.
The knights divided into two parties, one to besiege the tower, the
other to defend it, and the ladies awarded prizes to the victors. Thus the

audience found itself watching a richly costumed circus show, as elaborately conceived and as extravagantly performed as anything it was likely to see on the stage. Once again, this element could be happily adapted to the ballet, and we shall find plentiful examples of ritualised combat in the indoor spectacles at court.

The first French ballets were little more than a sequence of connected tableaux, enlivened and interwoven by songs and dances. We have a contemporary description of a masquerade performed at Bordeaux some time before 1576, in honour of Diane de Foix. It took place in the great hall of a private house. The only décor was an altar to the God of Love set up before the chimney-piece, and the characters made their entrance from the garden. First came the god Apollo, represented as having fallen in love with Diane, and singing a hymn of praise to the great power that held him captive. He was followed by Cupid himself, dressed in his traditional appurtenances. Then came four pilgrims to the shrine of love, bringing their gifts to the altar; and finally Diane herself, accompanied by four nymphs. A mock combat ensued in which Diane took Cupid prisoner and the nymphs, after a long struggle, subdued the pilgrims. Apollo abruptly took his leave, and Diane made a final triumphal entry in a chariot drawn by the four pilgrims.

Simple though it is, this seminal work already reveals most of the characteristics of the fully-developed court ballet. First, it is a strictly amateur performance, in which the leading personages of the household take major roles. We must remember, however, that these are amateurs who have been schooled in music and dance, as a necessary part of an upper-class education, from earliest childhood; who move with grace and dignity as a matter of course; and who can adapt their elaborate social dances to ballet roles at very short notice. Second, we may observe the setting. It is a simple example of a practice we shall see in more complex forms later on. A private room is adapted for performance by placing self-contained scenic units about the available space. Third, the theme: it is the basic conflict that we have observed in French tragedy, the war between the intellect and the passions, the power of the will and the temptations of the flesh, with, in this case, the will coming out firmly on top.

Such entertainments naturally suggested themselves for official court functions, where the allegory of the dance could make useful political propaganda. An early example was *Le Ballet Polonais*, presented in 1573 at the Palais des Tuileries for the entertainment and edification of a visiting Polish embassy. About one hour in length, it used as its central decorative motif a huge suspended clock, from which stepped down sixteen female figures representing the various provinces of France. They then performed a series of formation dances on the main floor. This ballet was the work of a distinguished group of collaborators. Ronsard provided the libretto, de Lassus the score, and the choreography was the work of an immigrant Italian who had been given an appointment as Superintendent of Music at the French court. Baptised Baldassarino di Belgioioso, he now assumed the French version of his name, Balthazar de Beaujoyeux, in honour of his adopted country; and he is unanimously hailed by dance historians as the true father of the French ballet.

Beaujoyeux's master work appeared a few years later, on 15 October 1581, in the Salle du Petit Bourbon in the Louvre, Commissioned to celebrate a royal marriage, the *Ballet Comique de la Reine* dwarfed every ballet that had gone before, and most that came after. *Comique* in this context did not, of course, imply comic; though the work had amusing interludes, its tone was generally serious. Rather, *comique* signified that the work involved spoken dialogue and a dramatic plot (*comédie*) as distinct from the pure dance interludes (*intermèdes*), just as *comédien* in French means not comedian but actor, and Bizet's tragic *Carmen* is classified as *opéra comique* because its original libretto contained substantial spoken passages. Beaujoyeux, who was prone to explain everything that he wrote, offered his own charming definition of the title: '*Comique* for the lovely, tranquil and happy conclusion by which it ends; by the quality of the personages involved, who are almost all gods and goddesses or other heroic persons. *Ballet*, because it is a geometrical arrangement of numerous people dancing together under a harmony of diverse instruments.' Once again, Beaujoyeux worked with a team of distinguished collaborators. Chemay wrote the lyrics, de Beaulieu the music, and Jacques de Patin, the King's Painter, created the sumptuous sets.

The Salle du Petit Bourbon was one of those enormous palace halls we have already noted. It was large enough for formation dances of great complexity, the so-called *danse horizontale*, making a kaleidoscopic sequence of geometrical figures on the floor – a kind of spectacle familiar to all who have enjoyed the evolutions of marching bands in American college football games. It was high enough for characters to be suspended in mid-air, and make descents from the designer's beloved flying machines. The royal dais was at one end of the hall at floor level, and surrounded by a select group of courtiers. Most of the audience, however, occupied galleries round the perimeter of the room, and looked down on the dances from above; they would thus have had a better view than the King. Directly opposite the royal throne stood the palace and enchanted garden of the sorceress Circe, luxuriantly decorated with exotic trees. Behind this hung a backdrop, a painted townscape. To the right was a wood, from which issued organ music; to the left, a 'golden vault' where more musicians were hidden. This disposition of the setting clearly looks back to the Middle Ages; the various scenic units are the 'mansions' of the religious drama brought into an enclosed space, in the same way that stage settings were created in the early days of the Hôtel de Bourgogne. But the new Italian influences in design are obvious also, both in the use of the painted perspective backdrop and the elaborate flying machines that dominate the action.

The theme of the ballet, set forth at great length by Beaujoyeux, was the return of the Golden Age. It was worked out in a plot based loosely on an episode in Homer's *Odyssey*, the encounter of Ulysses with the sorceress Circe, who enchanted his men and turned them into swine. Four acts were devoted to this, with intervening entries and dances (*intermèdes*) drawing on a wide range of more or less relevant characters from Greek mythology. The *corps de ballet* who performed in the *intermèdes* and the main action also served as costumed stage hands, drawing the elaborate floats and chariots into position. According to the usual rigid protocol, the entire thrust of the performance was directed towards the King, who found himself appealed to by the players, and by the end of the action, classed among the highest divinities of Olympus as a saviour of the oppressed and restorer of fallen fortunes.

The entertainment began with the appearance of the castaway Ulysses, running in fear from the enchantress Circe. In an exposition addressed directly to the royal throne, he begged for divine aid in his predicament:

> I would petition heaven to proclaim
> That the Age of Iron, so cruel, so inhumane,
> Might change for better; that the gods might come,
> By Saturn's side, to make this world their home,
> To live with mankind, and once more advance
> The cause of peace and plenty here in France.

He was followed by Circe, complaining furiously at the loss of her prey; and she in turn by the first of the self-contained *intermèdes*. This was a parade of major and minor aquatic deities – sirens, tritons and Nereids hauling a sea-shell chariot in which rode the goddess Thetys. After a dance, and a song voicing their own condemnation of the witch Circe, the group departed, leaving the floor clear for Act Two. Here the audience saw Circe practising her arts, and transforming a ballet of Nereids into statues. A cloud descended from the ceiling, revealing the winged god Mercury. He used his powers to free the Nereids, but fell victim to Circe in his turn; having enchanted him, she carried him off with the Nereids into her garden.

After the second *intermède,* a song and dance of satyrs playing on the flute, Act Three showed the various characters appealing to Pan, god of the woods and fields, to release his father Mercury. Revealed in his grotto by the falling of a curtain, Pan promised his aid. The third and final *intermède,* the entrance of the goddess Minerva in a flying chariot surrounded by the four Virtues, ushered in the parade of major deities who were to conclude the work. Minerva made her appeal first to the King and then to Jupiter, who descended from the ceiling in yet another flying cloud. Jupiter, Minerva and Pan combined to attack Circe's palace in a dance version of the mimic sieges of the old medieval tournaments. Circe was captured, Mercury delivered, and all the characters knelt in final homage to the King.

Again, this is a work in which the familiar motifs of French classical tragedy are duplicated in dance. The flattery of the monarch, as saviour, protector, and ultimate arbiter, is blatant. The political relevance is obvious. And in the allegorical representation of the enslavement of the nobler part of man by his baser passions, we see the themes soon to attract the attention of Corneille, Racine and their contemporaries in tragedy. Beaujoyeux makes this clear in his own interpretation. Circe, he tells us, is the daughter of the Sun and the Sea. Thus she represents the principle of change, growth and decay as embodied in the works of nature. In the physical world she controls the endlessly recurring cycle of the seasons, given visible form in the ballet by the convolutions of the Nereids' dance. In her psychological aspect she represents the sensual part of man, always in a state of flux and liable to sudden tempestuous change. Ulysses' sailors have become her captives, and been transformed into swine, because they have permitted their baser passions to triumph over the voice of pure reason. Thus, to combat Circe and all she stands for, other forces must be brought into play: the cardinal Virtues, the eloquence of Mercury, the wisdom of Minerva, the ultimate power of Jupiter and, of course, the King.

The *Ballet Comique de la Reine* was conspicuous consumption raised to the level of high art. It flattered the sponsors by demonstrating the extent of their purses – though in this case, the expenses were so enormous that rumblings were heard from the financial controllers, and no ballet ever cost quite so much again. It flattered the audience by assuming the extent of their wit and erudition, so that the court ballet, like the masque in England, the *noh* play in Japan, and other art forms of élitist societies, became a badge of class, to which the ticket of admission was one's ability to understand. Not that this deterred a mass of spectators who felt that presence at such events was a necessary prop to their social prestige; the records are full of the names of parvenus demanding invitations on the grounds that they had friends among the aristocracy. On one occasion, according to a slightly less than credible story, the royal party, entering a hall crammed to suffocation by would-be spectators, announced that the ballet was cancelled. After the crowd had dispersed, the dancers were summoned back to be enjoyed in private.

The art of the court ballet reached full maturity under Louis XIV, who bestowed his cachet of approval by enjoying it avidly and appearing in it personally, more often than not in women's roles. When he was only twelve years old he danced his first solo part, in *Cassandra*, and gave up dancing only at the age of thirty-one, either because of political sensitivity (according to the *Britannicus* story) or, more prosaically, because he had grown too stout. His presence naturally encouraged court participation at the highest levels, and funds were always available for the King's pleasures. His fellow dancers were still mainly noble amateurs, whose existing repertoire of stately social dances – saraband, allemand, minuet – could easily be deployed, in appropriate costume, for ballet purposes; and as these dances were still *horizontales*, the more advanced skills required for elevations were as yet unnecessary. Professionals, long familiar at the Italian courts, were only slowly and grudgingly admitted. They did not appear at the French court until 1630, and then only in comic, and thus undignified, roles. Not until 1659 were a favoured few allowed to share with the nobility the solemn dignity of the *grand ballet* which concluded every presentation. Finally, to match the reluctance with which the professional actress had been allowed to emerge in the theatre proper, the *première danseuse* was the last professional to appear in the ballet, both at court and on the commercial stage.

Ballets could be given anywhere the court happened to be. They did not have to be indoors, though this was easier for the contrivance of stage machinery and special effects. Open-air performances were equally popular, and given frequently in the châteaux of the great. One of the most famous, which involved both the rising star of Molière and the eclipse of a prominent minister, was held at Vaux-le-Vicomte, some thirty miles south-east of Paris, in the summer of 1661. This was the residence of Nicolas Fouquet, Minister of Finance. Louis XIV had long suspected that the magnificence of the Vaux château was supported by public funds, and now, as if insolently anxious to advertise the extent of his peculations, Fouquet invited the royal party to an entertainment far more splendid than he should have been able to afford. The fête concluded with a ballet and the inevitable fireworks display which blazoned Fouquet's presumptuous motto 'Quo non ascendam?' ('To what heights may I not rise?') across the night sky. This was the last straw for Louis, and France soon found herself under a new Minister of Finance. But the script of the ballet remains. Written by commission in the incredibly short time of two weeks, *Les Fâcheux* (*The Bores*) allowed Molière to direct the established art into new patterns, and brought him a string of such commissions thereafter. This was no political allegory but a more frivolous diversion, a *comédie-ballet* in which dance and dialogue were more closely integrated than had usually been the case.

The plot of *Les Fâcheux* is slight. It concerns a lover, Eraste, late for an appointment with his lady, and constantly detained by a succession of bores who thrust themselves upon him and trap him in tiresome conversation. There is no particular structure; the scenes could be arranged in any order and the chief interest is in the sharply-observed characters, whom the audience must have delighted in identifying with types of bores they all knew. The story is told that Louis, on leaving the ballet, pointed out a nobleman among the crowd and said to Molière 'You should have put *him* in it.' Molière manages to work off some of his own resentments: Eraste's opening monologue concerns a gentleman coming late to a play, shouting for a seat, finally sitting where he blocked the view of the stage for most of the *parterre*, and ruining the performance by gossiping with his neighbours throughout.

It was the relationship between the play and the ballet that was interestingly different. It began conventionally enough with the usual grandiose invocation, spoken in this case by Madeleine Béjart dressed as a water-nymph and emerging from a huge sea shell:

> I leave my cave, the deep that is my home,
> To see the greatest king the world has known.
> Must earth and sea then offer to your sight,
> To pleasure him, some yet unknown delight?
> That he should ask it should not come amiss:
> No reign has seen such miracles as his.

There is much more in the same unctuous vein. So far, all is normal. But the ballet interludes which follow are more strictly related to the plot. Drawn from observations of town and country life, they utilise players of *boule* and other games, gardeners and curious sightseers, who thrust themselves upon the major characters, involve them in their dances, make an effective bridge between scenes, and continue the theme of the play in dance action. It is the first example of a type of entertainment that Molière was profitably to exploit in his later career.

Determined not to be outdone by a mere minister, even one now fallen from grace, Louis promptly engaged on the construction of a new palace, destined to be the showplace of its own and subsequent ages, the background for the most elaborate of the royal ballets, and the place to which every actor, singer, artist and musician in Paris would have given his soul to be invited. As though determined to build as far away from Vaux as possible, he chose a site on the other side of Paris, to the north-west. This was Versailles, a place which had few immediately obvious attractions. Louis XIII had built a small hunting lodge there, which with time had grown into a small château; there was nothing else but a meagre collection of houses. Versailles, however, had a special place in Louis' heart. It was the scene of his frequent assignations with his current mistress, Louise de la Vallière; and the king who hated the Louvre now determined to transform it into a monument to his own power and splendour. His ministers protested, but in vain. Colbert, formerly Fouquet's assistant and now Minister of Finance in his place, threw up his hands in horror. The project was too extravagant, too expensive, and Colbert was a cautious man. Louis was adamant. Vaux-le-Vicomte, in a final act of victimisation, was plundered to embellish the new structure. New buildings started to rise: two large brick edifices, flanking the original château and embracing a courtyard to be known as the *cour royale*. An elaborate entrance lodge gave admission to the whole. Three pairs of symmetrical *pavillons* were provided to accommodate visiting courtiers, actors and musicians. Behind the château, the most gifted landscape artist of the century laid out lawns, walks, trees and fountains in symmetrical and regulated profusion.

The *pavillons* were soon in great demand. Whenever Louis took up residence, Versailles was a magnet that drew the highest of the land, and the finest performing talents in Paris. It did not matter that the lodgings were cramped, frigid and incommodious, or that courtiers were forced to squabble over attic rooms that servants would have despised elsewhere. To be at Versailles was to be in a state of grace; to be denied an invitation was social death. The nobility could happily endure the inconvenience. Under the new dispensations, their *raison d'être* was to dance attendance on the King, and they had nothing else to do. For the troupes of performers summoned, often at grotesquely short notice, to provide the entertainments, it was another story. Time shrinks distance, and we tend to minimise the difficulty even of routine journeys in earlier days. Today's visitor reaches Versailles from Paris quickly and easily; it is a half-hour ride in the little electric train from the bowels of the Invalides. In Molière's time, it was a four-hour journey over bumpy dirt roads on horseback. Not only had a constant supply of original plays and ballets to be devised, for the court had an insatiable appetite for novelty; these works had to be mounted and rehearsed in unpropitious surroundings, amid the thousand distractions of court life, and combined somehow with the everyday business of running a commercial playhouse in Paris. Yet the royal patronage could not be denied, and the players, despite the vexations, usually profited handsomely from the honour. Works created for Versailles could be fed back into the commercial theatre and presented, in however truncated a form, to audiences who delighted in vicariously sharing the experience of their monarch.

At least the formal elegance of Versailles offered a perfectly composed setting. Whether in the natural shelter of lawns, trees and fountains, or in theatres specially erected where the long walks crossed and joined, ample space could be found for actors, dancers, orchestras and mechanical fantasies. Even now, among the muted splendours of a Versailles turned into a museum, visitors may recapture a faint echo of these vanished, transitory delights. On certain evenings in the summer the grounds are thrown open for a *fête de nuit*. The public sprawls upon the grass, an unseen orchestra plays, and through the shimmer of fountains, glowing in the tinted light, dancers from the Opera perform their ballet, and the evening ends with fireworks.

How splendid the original occasions were we know by illustration and report. One description will suffice here, the lavish fête given in 1664 under the title of *Les Plaisirs de l'Ile Enchantée*. Ostensibly, this was in honour of the Queen. In reality, as the whole court knew, it celebrated the birth of the King's son to Louise de la Vallière – dragged from childbed to attend mass five hours later, to preserve some semblance of respectability. This issue of the previous December was now celebrated under brighter skies. Six hundred guests attended the week-long festivities, recorded for us in a series of engravings.

On the first evening, there was a procession of heroic characters from the works of Ariosto, whose poems were then much in vogue. It was virtually a ballet in itself, with the participants dressed in sumptuous versions of the tragic-heroic costumes familiar on the contemporary stage. Louis took part himself as the Knight Ruggiero, in a silver cuirass embroidered with gold and diamonds, and with flame-red plumes cresting his helmet. At nightfall, when the torches had been lit, the guests saw a parade of the seasons devised by Molière's company: Madeleine Béjart on a bear as Winter, Mlle du Parc on a colt as Spring, her husband on an elephant as Summer, La Thorillière as Autumn on a camel. Hard on their heels came a mechanical spectacle, a moving mountain on which were displayed Molière as Pan and his wife as the goddess Diana.

This was merely the prelude. Successive days brought more extravagant delights. Molière contributed *La Princesse d' Elide*, a five-act ballet spectacle composed in the desperate hurry to which he was by then resigned. The measure of his haste may be seen in the text; starting out in verse, it lapses after the beginning of the second act into prose. As usual, the plot was skimpy, dealing with a princess who despised all lovers until she was vanquished by a suitor who turned the tables by pretending to disdain her. Performed in a specially-constructed theatre protected by hangings, *La Princesse* relied for its effect on sheer spectacle: *un spectacle de Folies-Bergère*, as one critic has called it. There were choruses of satyrs and valets, crowds of peasants, packs of hounds; Armande played the Princess, and Molière, in what seems to have been one of his most athletic performances, the Court Jester.

Another entertainment, staged in the great meadow, offered a ballet in the round, centred on the scenic palace of the witch Alcina. Any work involving sorcery was bound to be prolific of monsters. Armande, dancing the role of a nymph, entered on the back of a mechanical whale, so realistically contrived that many spectators were prepared to swear that it had been fished out of the sea and brought straight to Versailles for the occasion. As the ballet closed, the palace was consumed by fireworks. *Les Fâcheux* was successfully revived, and only one of Molière's works cast a shadow over the event. This was the first performance of a short version of his *Tartuffe*, which carried such obvious potentialities for offence that it was almost immediately banned from the public stage, and started a controversy that endured for years. The *Tartuffe* incident, however, did not diminish Molière's prestige as a composer of ballets for the court; he was to continue this kind of work almost until his death, though more and more with collaborators who eventually elbowed him out of fashion.

Elitist art seldom outlives its time, and works composed for the moment rarely desire or deserve a longer life. Today's classics were yesterday's popular successes, designed to appeal to a broad range of humanity and thereby extending their impact in time as well as in their own place. Works composed for cliques rarely survive the audience they were meant for. It might therefore seem that the court ballet hardly deserves to be considered as a serious contribution to dramatic art. Like the court masque in contemporary England, it was part of the final efflorescence of the absolute power of the monarch. Depending on royal subsidy for its development and support, it represented an added dimension of a ceremonial court life in which costumes, manners and movement were scarcely less rigidly prescribed, or less rigorously rehearsed, than in their scripted counterparts in the ballet. Court life and court art were hardly distinguishable. Changing manners brought about the ballet's death. Even in the later years of Louis XIV, a more pious mistress and a straitened economy turned the King away from the spectacles he had once adored. Though Louis XV's Versailles acquired a charming permanent indoor theatre, it seems never to have been used. In England, when Charles I was driven from his throne by the Puritan revolt, he left behind a huge half-finished masque-house, torn down before it could be completed. Although many of the scripts and much of the music survives, the masques and ballets can never be revived in the spirit which created them, even if an audience could be found to understand and enjoy them.

Yet though the world of the ballet was so narrowly contained, it has clear affinities with the other theatrical arts of the time. It both borrowed from them and spilled over onto them; and beneath its decorative surface it may be seen to be motivated by the same principles. We have already noted how ballet, like tragedy, went back to the classics for inspiration and subject matter, and how the handling of the basic themes was similar, if not identical. The conflict between reason and the passions is the all-purpose theme of a professedly rationalist age. It produces a diversity of plots, and can be expressed just as cogently in the sparse language of Racinian tragedy at the Hôtel de Bourgogne, or in the decorative flourishes of a tableau showing Hercules enchained by Love at the Court of Savoy. Perhaps less obvious is the way in which the controlled manipulations of the dance respond to the same patterns that shape the interactions of the characters in tragedy – or, as we shall later see, in comedy. Step matches step just as verse responds to verse; an advance on one side is answered by a retreat on the other; the shifting geometric patterns of tragic action, such as those suggested for *Phèdre* in the previous chapter, are given visible form in the ballet. Molière is credited with a dance-work called *The Ballet of Incompatibles*, which matched various unlikely pairs and exploited the contrast between them; in many ways his light and serious comedies can be seen to do the same thing.

In its side-effects ballet had a clear influence on the contemporary stage. Molière's work in this field led him to evolve, for popular consumption, a form of comedy in which dance played an important part, and where ballet episodes were interwoven into the main action, commenting and embroidering upon the narrative content of the scenes and translating them into a different mode. We shall consider a major example of this, Le Bourgeois Gentilhomme, in the next chapter. It is important to remember that a good deal of Molière's work was conceived with dance in mind; that, in a play like The Miser, the scenes were intended to be interspersed with ballet interludes; and that in modern productions, seeing, as we usually do, the dramatic element alone, purged of dance, we are left with only a partial vision of the piece. Molière without dance is like Greek tragedy without music. In both cases we have grown so familiar with the deficient versions that we have to keep reminding ourselves of what we are missing.

Side by side with the court ballet there also emerged the beginnings of opera and classical ballet as we now know them, borrowing courtly scenes and devices and in many cases using the same personnel. Opera was already known in Italy, and now began to attract admirers on both sides of the Channel. In England, during the last, ill-fated years of Charles I, Sir William D'Avenant, a far-sighted and unscrupulous theatrical entrepreneur, secured a patent allowing him to present Italian opera in London. Theatrical monopolies, as we have already seen in the case of the Hôtel de Bourgogne, were the pattern of the age; and though D'Avenant's project was frustrated by the Civil War, it showed the direction of the future. In France, a parallel development took place. Paul Perrin, a Lyonnais born in 1625, is regarded as the creator of French opera. An abbé of classical learning and considerable literary ability – he had already translated Vergil's Aeneid into French verse – he composed a Pastorale, set to music by his friend Cambert, which has passed into history as the first French musical comedy. Cardinal Mazarin esteemed this work highly enough to have it played for the court at Vincennes, and Perrin went on to other classically-inspired musical entertainments, Ariadne and Bacchus, and The Death of Adonis. Emboldened by success he proposed the foundation of an official Academy of Music, and eventually obtained the exclusive right to stage opera in Paris in imitation of the Italian style.

This was a potential goldmine, but Perrin was not a sufficiently astute businessman to profit from it. Swindled by his associates and brought to the verge of bankruptcy, he finally surrendered his interest to a man who had already shown himself adept in sharp dealing. This was Jean Baptiste Lully, a jack-of-all-trades in the arts but best known as a composer of opera and ballet. Originally christened Giovanni Battista, Lully was a Florentine, one of the many Italians who found a profitable career in the French theatre. Presented at court in 1642, he became the *valet de chambre* of Louise d' Orléans, cousin to the King. In the same year the young Molière was meditating his first onslaught on the Paris theatre; the careers of the two Jean Baptistes were to become closely intertwined. Ten years later, having left the Orléans household (not apparently without some stain on his character), Lully appeared in the court orchestra of Louis XIV, where he quickly established a reputation, not merely as a violin virtuoso, but as a dancer of professional ability. In rapid succession he became the leader of a twenty-four-piece orchestra, court composer and, in 1661, Superintendent of the Queen's Music. He owed his advancement not so much to his professional skill, considerable though this was, but rather to the fact that he was a consummate and unscrupulous politician. Working in his adopted French, he created a number of works for court performance, particularly distinguishing himself in the *Ballet de la Nuit*, where he danced five roles in a thirteen-hour extravaganza. The young Louis also danced in this work, and Lully speedily won the royal favour. Louis was fascinated by him, in spite of his unprepossessing appearance, and the combination of offices that Lully eventually secured for himself gave him virtual control of music in France. In 1672 he found it easy to manoeuvre Perrin from his privileged operatic position and buy him out in return for a pension.

Though he worked with Molière on a number of occasions, in particular composing the music for *Le Bourgeois Gentilhomme* and creating the role of the Grand Mufti in it, Lully tried to put that playwright too out of business, complaining that it was an infringement of his new rights for anyone else to produce *comédie-ballet*. His own work was to be seen everywhere in Paris while other theatres were prohibited from using more than a token number of musicians. This meant, among other things, the death of the Marais, which was then relying on musical and mechanical spectacle to woo back a fickle public. Even a marionette theatre suffered from Lully's displeasure: the *Troupe Royale des Pygmées* was suppressed because the puppets were presenting opera. When Molière died in 1673, his company, now headed by his widow Armande, was evicted from the Palais-Royal that had been their home for so many years, and forced to seek accommodation elsewhere: Lully promptly took over the theatre as an opera house. Having finally negotiated himself into the ranks of the nobility, he died in 1687 as a result of a bizarre accident. Energetically flourishing his long baton, he stabbed himself in the foot. Blood poisoning set in, and the wound proved fatal. There must have been many in Paris who did not mourn his passing.

One of Lully's associates in the all-powerful Academy of Music and Dance was Pierre Beauchamp, descended from a line of violinists but, like Lully, also a dancer of repute. In 1664 he had appeared in the first full collaboration between Lully and Molière at Versailles; the accounts show that he was paid fifty *louis d'or* for his services. His chief contribution, however, was not as a performer but as an innovator in dance technique. Court ballet, as we have seen, tended to be limited in its movements and positions. It contained more patterned marching than what we should now call choreography proper, and the ballet master served rather as a pageant master. Beauchamp belongs to the period in which the wider use of the body was being explored, and in which dance began to involve vertical as well as horizontal movement. This change was largely enforced upon the ballet by its shift of location. Once the dancers moved out of the great halls at court, where most of the spectators looked down on the performance from above, to the raised stage of the commercial theatre, ballet conceived purely in terms of horizontal formations was no longer possible. In this development of verticality and elevation Beauchamp played a major part. He defined the five basic positions that have become the foundation of our ballet, and is also credited with developing the first system of dance notation. In these various ways, the court arts inspired much that would become familiar in the later popular theatre. Just as in England the commercial theatre of the Restoration was heavily influenced by audience memories of pre-war court masques, so the eighteenth-century theatre of France owed much to the spectacles at the Louvre and Versailles.

One other affiliate of the court ballet must be considered here: the machine-play, beloved particularly of the Marais but known to other theatres also, which relied on much of the same sort of spectacle for its effect. This genre of drama had its own particular rewards and problems. As we have seen, stage settings in the commercial theatre of this period tended normally to an extreme simplicity. We have an interesting confirmation of this in the contracts and correspondence of a French troupe invited to Stockholm in 1699. They were to occupy two theatres of the kind familiar in France: one a hall in the royal castle, the other a converted *jeu de paume*. The visitors were required by contract to fur-

nish their own settings for the latter. As it turned out, only three basic
sets were necessary for the whole of the existing repertory: the inevitable *palais à volonté* for tragedy; a formal garden-landscape, for tragic
and other exteriors; and a *salon* interior to serve for virtually all of
Molière's comedies. The list of properties was also of the simplest. It is
a significant comment on the size of French theatres that when Paris-
built sets were shipped to Stockholm, they turned out to be far too
small; it was complained that they barely covered the walls.

The machine plays created a different set of problems, for their appeal
lay much less in thought and language – the plots tend to be trivial,
and the dialogue is hardly profound – and much more in sheer spectacle.
Into this genre were poured all the mechanical inventiveness and
exuberant love of show that found no outlet in the regular repertoire.
Such inventiveness had been present in the French theatre since the
Middle Ages; the reader may recall the description of the Bourges play
in Chapter 1, with its graphically depicted shipwreck, flagellations and
beheadings, and the elaborate mechanical tableaux of Heaven and Hell.
It received a tremendous boost, however, from explorations conducted
in Renaissance Italy, which stemmed, curiously enough, from a desire
to reconstruct the theatres of classical Greece and Rome. So far, we have
seen the effects of this classical revival mainly in the simplicity that
was urged upon the French drama. We now see the other side of the
coin; for though most modern scholars now consider Greek play production to have been a fairly simple business, relying largely on the
spoken word and the power of suggestion to create its effects, the contemporaries of Shakespeare and Molière were just as convinced that in
some aspects it was very elaborate indeed. Though written considerably
after our period, the article on *Machines du théâtre* in Diderot's
Encyclopédie still gives an accurate summary of contemporary scholarly
thinking on the subject: 'The ancients possessed, as we do, three kinds
of stage machines in general: one kind, which did not permit descents,
but simply moved across the theatre; a second, in which the gods
descended to stage level from aloft; and a third, which was used to raise
or support characters in mid-air in an illusion of flight.' Renaissance
scholars, in attempting to revive the form and spirit of the ancient
drama, had claimed to find evidence for such machinery in the descriptions given by Vitruvius of the Roman theatre and Pollux of the Greek.
Both of these were late writers who described a decadent classical
theatre that had indeed lapsed into a love of spectacle for its own sake,
and the accounts of stage machinery given in their works are garbled
and incomplete. The Renaissance designers, however, unhesitatingly

assumed that what was true of the late classical theatre was true of the whole, and started to translate their ancient sources into practical stage terms.

Thus the exploitation of stage machinery, founded on a dubious classical base, proliferated. Text books began to appear describing in detail, with diagrams, how to create various special effects. Sebastiano Serlio, who wrote a treatise on architecture in 1545 partially based on Vitruvius, laid out a system for instantaneously transforming a stage picture by the use of three-faced revolving scenic units. With a different design on each face, one painted setting could dissolve into another before the eyes. This device is still occasionally used in the modern theatre, and has found a new lease of life in the huge changing billboards familiar in our advertising. It was used for some time in the French theatre; there is even a record of five-faced units (one for each act?) being used at Nantes in 1586. It tended to be replaced, in the time of Corneille and Molière, by flat wing pieces rigged to slide in and out. Probably the French stage had less room for bulky units than the theatres of the Italian courts. Nevertheless the exciting possibilies of the magically changing stage picture had been established, and it was mechanically simple to supply a system whereby one set of wings and borders could be slid out of view, and another set in, by an adroit application of ropes and pulley.

The glory of the French stage was its flying machines – often literally a 'glory' showing a cloud-haloed deity in the heavens. This too had been approved medieval usage, particularly in the indoor Italian religious spectacles where overhead machinery could more easily be hung. Nicolas Sabattini in his *Manual for Constructing Theatrical Scenes and Machines* (1638) described a number of methods for showing clouds descending from the heavens, with or without people in them. They could be lowered on ropes from the ceiling; they could be attached to a horizontal beam that slid down a slot in the back scene; or they could be fastened to a long, counterweighted beam working like a derrick from a pivot on the floor. By a multiplication of such devices clouds could be made to appear to grow in size, or to split in the middle.

Aquatic effects were also much in demand. Waves gentle or tempestuous could be shown by profiles cut out and mounted on rollers at the rear of the stage. Turn the drums slowly, and you had a gentle swell; turn them fast, and you had a storm at sea. Ships could be shown as cut-outs and moved on slots and rollers through the waves. Sabattini even gives instructions on how to make a sea monster spouting water from the top of its head.

These were the kinds of effects that crammed the machine play. It followed that the *machiniste*, the man who constructed and controlled such devices, was a skilled technician, an expert in his own field. Diderot's *Encyclopédie*, illustrating the various sciences and industries, gives the construction of stage machinery an equal place among more sober trades. Certainly it involved no less mechanical skill. Some designers were visitors from abroad, like the Italians Torelli and Vigarani, who devised many of the effects for the court ballet and worked for other theatres also. The Marais in its later days had its own resident *machiniste*. Sometimes machines constructed for a private performance could be reused in the commercial theatre. Such was the case with Corneille's *Le Conquête de la Toison d'Or* (*The Capture of the Golden Fleece*), conceived originally for a ducal château with settings by the court painter Bellot, and later bequeathed to the Marais. Machines designed for one production could be converted for others. In the light of what has been said about the smallness of French theatres, it may seem strange that such elaborate devices could be used on the commercial stage at all. Certainly even at the Marais space was at a premium; although there was an 'upper stage' which could be used for celestial effects, this was diminutive, scarcely more than a large shelf overhanging the main floor. Obviously, however, the theatres achieved miracles of compression. Some idea of the possibilities available even within a small compass can be had from the Swedish court theatre of Drottningholm, still in use today as a living museum of the theatre arts of the past. Though built later than the period we are considering, Drottningholm embodied, and still displays in motion, the kinds of devices familiar to audiences at the Marais. Complete sets of baroque scenery have been preserved, together with the machinery that gave them life, and audiences may still see, either in the theatre itself or preserved on film, the full elaboration of opera at the time. The stage is minute. Even the principals have little room for movement, and the chorus is virtually restricted to a straight line, but the scenery gives a performance of its own. At the turn of a winch columns are replaced by trees, the backscene opens to reveal another view, waves roll, a ship sails, and the gods make their precarious cloud-girt descent from heaven.

Let us conclude with a description of one machine play, Corneille's *The Capture of the Golden Fleece* already mentioned. Corneille had already written a tragic *Medea*, recreating the versions of Euripides and Seneca for the French stage. *The Golden Fleece* goes back to an earlier episode in the same familiar story, Jason's quest for the fabulous treasure and his romantic involvements in Medea's land of Colchis. In common with tragedy it has the conventional five-act structure and the lengthy rhetoric. Belonging more to the ballet world are the elaborate settings and the mechanical divertissements which conclude each act.

The play opens with a prologue in the form of a political allegory. This has nothing to do with the main action. Characters representing France and Victory engage in a dialogue. Then 'the heavens open, to reveal Mars in a menacing attitude, one foot in the air, the other resting on his planet'. Mars is keeping Peace prisoner in his castle, displayed to the audience in another scenic discovery as a formidable place 'with columns made of cannons, mortars for the column bases, and cannon balls for capitals'. Peace is released from her confinement and brought down to earth. At her command, the gloomy palace is transformed into a luminous garden, and the play proper begins.

Corneille gives long descriptions of the stage settings. The garden belongs to Aietes, Medea's father; it is part of the royal palace. It has three ranks of cypress trees, statues and fountains; the whole is cut off by an *arcade de verdure*, backed by a landscape in painted perspective. At the end of the act this prospect is further brightened by the first mechanical entrée. Iris enters on her rainbow, accompanied by Juno and Pallas in separate chariots. This show of goddesses obviously involved some tricky rope-work: 'As Iris disappears, Pallas simultaneously rises into the heavens, and Juno sinks into the earth, both traversing the length of the stage as they go, and passing each other in their chariots'.

In Act Two the garden disappears, to be replaced by a river with rocky banks. The entrée here is an aquatic spectacle: the river-god Glaucus rises from the river's depths accompanied by singing sirens and tritons, 'while a great shell of mother-of-pearl, encrusted with branches of coral and precious stones, carried by four dolphins and kept aloft by four winds in mid-air, comes to a gradual halt in the middle of the same river.' Act Three gives us another palace scene: 'Our theatre has so far revealed no spectacle so brilliant as the palace of King Aietes, which serves as the decoration for this act.' It has flanking rows of jasper columns and golden statues. But an angry Medea transforms it, with one blow of her magic wand, into a 'palace of horror'. In its place, we see columns shaped like ferocious beasts: elephants, rhinoceroses, lions, ounces, tigers, leopards, panthers, dragons and serpents, all with a menacing appearance. From a dark grotto, four winged monsters advance on Medea's rival in love, and threaten to devour her. But she is saved by a cloud 'which descends almost to earth. It divides into two parts which disappear into the wings', revealing Absyrtus, Medea's brother, between them.

Act Four, less alarming, shows 'the desert where Medea is accustomed to retire to prepare her enchantments', covered with rocks and withered trees. This is enlivened by a 'panorama of Venus' palace, showing the God of Love in flight – not from side to side, but directly towards the spectators, something never done in the French theatre up to this time.' And finally, in Act Five, 'a thick forest composed of interlaced trees, the Forest of Mars.' Shields and weapons hang from the branches, with the Golden Fleece fastened to one of the trees. When Jason has achieved his quest, the play closes with the most magnificent spectacle of all: 'The heavens open to reveal the palace of the Sun, who is seen in his luminous chariot advancing towards the spectators. Leaving his palace, he ascends to address Jupiter, whose own palace opens a moment later.' There sit Jupiter and Juno to preside over the grand finale, he with an eagle and a thunderbolt at his feet, she with a peacock.

In the history of the Marais and the career of Corneille, we see the diversity of the French theatre. The same stage that had contained smart social comedy, the romantic tragedy of *Le Cid*, and Corneille's later, more austere tragedies, held at the end of its life spectacles that bid fair to rival the displays at court.

7 The Craft of Comedy: Two Plays by Molière

Molière's genius ranged almost as wide as Corneille's. Though he never, so far as we know, wrote formal tragedy, he acted in it, and some of his darker, more introspective comedies have enough of the tragic spirit to contribute to the myth that Corneille had a hand in their composition. We have seen his activities as company manager, and as librettist and entrepreneur for the ballet spectacles at court. But it was for his comedies that Molière was most famous in his time, and his name has become synonymous with French comedy ever since. It is sufficient testimony to his genius that his works are virtually the only comedies from the period to survive in the living theatre repertory. His contemporaries and rivals, limp and lacklustre by comparison, are preserved mainly in scholarly memory or in occasional academically-inspired revivals. Always controversial in his own time, sometimes hated, sometimes ridiculed, Molière came to represent, for later ages, the perfection of a particular comic style and the summation of an era of French social history.

French comedy in general, and Molière's in particular, had diverse roots. A native form of dramatic humour had flourished since the Middle Ages. Originating in the damp, cold north, where life was hard and opportunities to relieve the tedium of everyday existence were few, this peasant comedy turned an unsentimental eye on the inevitabilities of the daily round: scratching a living, hard bargaining, marriage, sickness, death. This hard material attitude to life lives on in the plays of Molière, where flights of romantic fancy are often tempered by a sense of the practical realities. Though we tend to think of the medieval drama largely in religious terms, there was a substantial secular tradition too, sometimes finding expression in bizarre ways. We would not think of the Dance of Death as a subject for comedy, but there seems to have been such a play, performed in Paris and echoing the famous frescoes of the Cemetery of the Innocents. The best known comedy of the period, *Pierre Pathelin*, celebrates an accomplished swindler, and evokes scenes familiar to the audience from their own experience in lawcourt and market-place.

Overshadowed by the religious plays, and thus less amply recorded – scholars have always been prone to ignore popular entertainment – these farces nevertheless flourished in the streets of Paris. Short comedies were played by groups of amateurs, particularly law-students, who ran riot on feast days and holidays and performed with all the uninhibited gusto of a student rag. Professional *farceurs* began to invade the Paris stage, first playing barely tolerated comic interludes between the serious perform-ances but soon, by popular demand, dominating the theatre. At the lowest point in its fortunes the Confrérie de la Passion found that audiences would still pay good money to see its resident comedians, the endearingly bawdy grotesques, their faces smeared with flour, who were the vaudeville clowns of the day. Their slapstick passed into the reper-toire of popular comedy; Molière, as actor, belonged to the same tradi-tion.

The native comedians, however, had more sophisticated, cosmopolitan rivals. One of these was the rediscovery of classical comedy, for even in its lighter mood the French stage sought to borrow prestige from the past. This did not mean Greek comedy, represented for the French, as still almost entirely for us, by the work of Aristophanes. His plays, though known, were neither well understood nor easily adaptable. To an age brought up to revere order and precision as classical virtues, they appeared formless and anarchic. Ranging from high poetry to obscene farce, from fantasy to mythology and social satire, they did not fall into any well-defined category. Their humour seemed too topical, even parochial; and the political and social involvement of Aristophanic comedy, built on the free and easy rapport between actors and audience in the Greek theatre, could not easily be recreated on a stage that had assumed a different shape, or for an audience inhibited by a different relationship between the government and the governed. Racine, for his one excursion into comedy, attempted to reproduce an Aristophanic play. This was *Les Plaideurs* (*The Litigants*). It had some success in Racine's time, and is occasionally revived today. But when one compares it to Aristophanes' original, *The Wasps*, the difference is glaringly apparent. Though the plots are substantially the same, all the earthiness and vitality have gone. And above all the chorus has gone; the comedy has become attenuated, polite. Aristophanes had much in common with Rabelais. They spoke the same comic language, and would have enjoyed each other. But in a theatre grown newly decorous, Aristophanes had no place.

For the French writers, therefore, classical comedy meant by necessity the Romans Plautus and Terence, a total of twenty-six plays themselves deriving from the Greek, but from a Greece a century later than Aristophanes, escapist plays, written for a wider audience and so dealing with more general subjects. Set in a comfortable, bourgeois world, they were built on a limited number of universally applicable, easily comprehended plots: the conflict of the generations, stern father versus scapegrace son; mistaken identities, and long-lost children; young love, surviving various improbable complications to arrive at an obligatory happy ending. These all-purpose plots, easily reshuffled into new combinations, were peopled by characters equally stereotypical, whose names might change from play to play but whose nature and behaviour never varied: angry old man, jolly old man, young playboy, cunning slave, stupid slave, each with his appropriate mask, language and stage business. There was no subtle interplay of character; humour arose from a clash of contrasting types, brought into conflict by the blind force of chance – always the prime mover in this sort of comedy – or the manipulations of a complex scheme dreamed up by one of the characters.

Plautus left twenty such plays, which rarely rise above this simple, though deft, mechanical level. Terence's six employ the same basic plots and characters but attempt a rather deeper psychological insight. Terence was also prone to pithy moralising, which kept his plays in favour after their commercial stage life had ended. They survived the general eclipse of classical drama in the Christian era and were never completely lost sight of, even in the Middle Ages. Plautus, dismissed as a mere popular entertainer and a man of no morals besides, had largely disappeared from view. His work was spectacularly rediscovered in the Renaissance, and as spectacularly revived, with a lavishness of staging that he would never have dreamed of. The Roman comedies thus took on a new lease of life, as part of the revival of interest in the classical stage. Playwrights were attracted to them, because they provided a number of simple models to follow. The stock characters of Roman comedy began to appear in new dresses on the stages of France and Italy, England and Spain.

The French did not have to look far to see a living example of this kind of comedy, vigorous and flourishing. This was the Italian comedy which had come to birth in the sixteenth century and, by Molière's time, had an international reputation: the *commedia dell' arte*, 'professional comedy', as distinct from the classically-inspired productions by enthusiastic amateurs. The *commedia* was essentially a people's theatre. It made no pretensions to intellectual eminence, claimed no profundity;

indeed, it thumbed its nose at such things. Yet it displayed its own classical affinities. The spirit of the *commedia* was essentially the spirit of Plautus and Terence. The plots and characters were the same, though played with a contemporary accent. In constructing a family tree for the *commedia*, we must proceed with caution. Theatre historians are prone to find influences where there are only similarities; it is the occupational disease of the profession. As human nature tends to remain constant, types of human folly reach across the centuries; in devising stock characters, the Romans and the *commedia* may easily have come to the same discoveries independently. Nevertheless, there are enough similarities to suggest that the Roman seed, having lain dormant in the soil of its own country for centuries, now produced a new crop of comic invention. The Roman stock characters reappeared with distinctive Italian regional affinities. The angry old father, Pantalone, was dressed as a caricature of a Venetian merchant: black cloak over tight red costume, black skull cap on a fringe of white hair. His common foil and companion was a pompous and pedantic man of letters, *il Dottore* – usually represented as a Doctor of Law from Bologna, Italy's oldest university, and dressed in academic black, with a long cloak and a broad-brimmed hat.

Two regular characters derived from the city of Bergamo. These were the servants Arlecchino and Brighella, recalling the inventive, lying slaves who, in Roman comedy, usually masterminded the preposterous plots. Arlecchino, eventually translated to the English theatre as Harlequin, began his stage life as a scarecrow figure, dressed in a costume patched all over with scraps of various colours. In time, this became refined into Harlequin's familiar diamond pattern. Brighella, in a baggy costume, was traditionally slower witted; though still a rogue, he served as foil to Arlecchino's quicksilver wit. There was a whole range of comic servants on which the comedies might draw – Truffaldino, Scapino, Pedrolino, others, each with his distinctive accent and behaviour. One recurrent character was deliberately given a foreign cast. This was *il Capitano*, the comic soldier, whose antecedents may be found in the fire-eating generals of Aristophanes and the *miles gloriosus* of Plautus. The *commedia* made him a Spaniard, taking an opportunity to pay off old resentments; they had grown too familiar with Spanish mercenaries in their interminable little wars. Full of strange oaths and jangling with equipment the Spanish captain came charging repeatedly onto the stage, only to retreat as soon as there was a prospect of real action. The English theatre knows him well. He has been reincarnated for us as Falstaff.

The *commedia* had one other feature in common with its presumptive Roman ancestors. Most of its characters wore masks. These fixed and defined each part within its appropriate range of language, behaviour and emotions. To this extent, the character existed without the actor. It resided in the mask and costume, which by tradition and habituation had come to confer their own personality on the man who wore them. An individual interpreter might contribute to the repertoire of his character's business. He might play the part better or worse. But he dared not, at his peril, trespass on another character's psychic territory. Each was distinct. Humour came, as in the Roman plays, when this panoply of grotesques was brought into collision. Significantly, the only unmasked *commedia* figures were the 'straight' characters, the romantic leads, who gave these antics the vestige of a connected plot. This was theatre, not life. The mask conferred theatrical reality, while unmasked characters were pushed into the background. For us, living in the twentieth century, the phenomenon is familiar from the Marx Brothers films, which are *commedia dell' arte* reborn on celluloid. It is the masks, the drolls, Groucho, Chico and Harpo, who come to urgent life on the screen. Zeppo, the straight man, the romantic songster, is easily forgettable and immediately forgotten.

Commedia dell' arte belongs to the category that Peter Brook has defined as 'rough' theatre: scriptless, often apparently formless, springing not from the mind of a literary creator but from some wellspring of achetypal comic behaviour. These were improvised plays, not in the sense that every moment was the result of spontaneous comic invention, but rather implying that the actors were free to elaborate, as their mood and that of the audience suggested, around an agreed plot-line. The scenario was established in advance. To this the performers added scenes, sight-gags and dialogues from a repertory of stage business which had evolved through generations. Long accustomed to playing together and working as a professional, if not indeed a real family, the actors learned to read one another's minds, and respond immediately to a given cue. They held in memory vast stores of business which could be immediately brought into action. In the surviving scenarii, the merest indication is enough: 'Here Arlecchino performs the *lazzi* of the chamberpot.' These *lazzi* (the technical word for episodes of comic business) were the *commedia* actor's vocabulary, out of which he shaped each individual performance. This is the immemorial language of pure theatre, spoken by the Graeco-Roman mimes, by Garrick as Harlequin, by the red-nosed, bladder-wielding comics of American burlesque, and by the Chaplin of the silent films.

For the *commedia*, it was primarily a physical language. Visual, acrobatic comedy was the mainstay of such pieces. The touring companies often found themselves playing for audiences who could not speak Italian; in Paris, indeed, they were for some time forbidden to speak in French. Even in Italy, peasant audiences had no great fondness for literary wit. But the language of sign and gesture could always communicate. As in ballet, the body spoke a universal tongue. In the case of the *commedia*, it was often a coarse tongue. Though remarkably free of sexual humour, the *commedia* found the grosser bodily functions irresistibly amusing. The chamber pot and, above all, the anal enema, were props in constant demand.

The Italian companies ranged throughout Europe. They were in Germany and Holland, Sweden and France; their pantomimic versatility recognised no frontiers, and wherever they went they left their mark on the native tradition. In France, they had already been welcome visitors for many years. Cherished at court level, they were also adored by the masses. Tragedy was 'official art', but the Italian farces, robust, inventive, unpretentious, spoke to everyone. The first official appearance of an Italian troupe in France is recorded in 1548, before Henri II and Catherine de Medici at Lyons. Though this invited company performed a scripted play, it was rapidly followed by others offering the more exuberant improvised material. Henri III, who may have seen the *commedia* on its home ground in Venice, invited the famous Gelosi company to Blois in 1576. From there they went on to Paris, where they met the inevitable difficulties of any company trying to shake the Confrérie's monopoly. Nevertheless, though a succession of legal obstacles was placed in their way, the Italian companies in Paris multiplied under royal favour. From 1600 to 1604 the Gelosi, under the patronage of Henri IV, played regularly at the Hôtel de Bourgogne. They were followed by the equally famous Fedeli, and they in turn by the troupe of Giuseppe Bianchi, which included one actor of particular note. This was Tiberio Fiorilli, famous for his interpretation of Scaramouche, and Molière's legendary 'tutor'. According to the stories, Molière was a regular attender at his performances, or even received formal lessons from him. Certainly there was a close association in their later careers. Fiorelli's troupe had been installed in the Petit Bourbon in 1655, and was still there three years later, when Molière returned from the provinces. For a while the two companies shared a theatre, playing on alternate days. The story of Molière's tutelage is metaphorically, if not factually, true. Molière's early comedies are Italian plays in French dress. They show the extensive influence upon him of *commedia* performances either observed in Paris or met on the road during his thirteen-year provincial exile. It is the strongest single influence upon him; and, arguably, it never completely left him.

Disregarding the vexed question of the 'lost' plays, we may see, from Molière's earliest extant work, how extensive this influence was. In *Le Médecin Volant* (*The Flying Doctor*), one of the first plays we have, Molière takes an Italian plot, and unabashedly dresses it in Italian characters and business. The story is of the slightest. It concerns a servant who masquerades as a doctor to help a young girl cheat her father and marry the man she really loves. Though the characters have French names, their Italian origins shine through them. The crotchety old father, Gorgibus, stern but infinitely gullible, is our old friend Pantalone. His crony, a man of law, is *Il Dottore*, the Comic Professor. The servant masquerading as a doctor of medicine gives us a variant of the same type. The servant himself, Sganarelle, is the archetypal rogue of the *commedia*, quick-tongued, nimble-witted and ever resourceful in deception. *Le Médecin Volant* is in fact designed as a *tour de force* for the actor who plays this part – originally Molière himself, almost certainly, though we have no firm evidence. It calls for him to appear alternately as the servant and the fake doctor, switching from one to the other with increasing rapidity as the play proceeds. Finally, both servant and doctor are supposed to be in the same room, talking through the window to the father outside. This calls for meticulous timing, acrobatic dexterity and lightning changes of costume, the sort of thing that Molière, as actor, was to delight in all his life.

Though the derivation of the plot is clear, in the matter of stage business it is always difficult to say who borrows what from whom. Comic ideas cannot be copyrighted, and performers of every age have helped themselves liberally to one another's material. Molière was no exception to the general rule. '*Je prends mon bien où je le trouve*,' he is reputed as saying: 'If I find something I can use, I take it.' The Italians were no less prone to borrow, and the *commedia* and French companies working side by side in Paris must have been mutually influential. Nevertheless, our knowledge of the *lazzi* suggests that Molière took over a good deal of the traditional business and censored it slightly, playing against the expected vulgarity, rather in the style of a seventeenth-century Frankie Howerd, to give the familiar material a different twist. A well-known *commedia* joke, for example, is the man tricked into drinking urine thinking that it is wine. In the following sequence Sganarelle reverses the joke:

GORGIBUS	Sabine, run along and fetch a sample of my daughter's urine. Oh, doctor, I'm afraid she's going to die!
SGANARELLE	She'd better not! A fine thing, dying without the doctor's orders! Ah, here comes the urine. This indicates some heating and inflammation of the intestines. (*Tasting it*) However, it's not all that bad.
GORGIBUS	What! You're tasting it!
SGANARELLE	Don't be so surprised. Most doctors are satisfied with looking at it. But I'm no ordinary doctor. I drink it, because it tells me a lot about the cause and progress of the disease. But to tell you the truth, there's not enough here for a reasonable diagnosis. Tell her to piss a bit more.
SABINE	I had a lot of trouble getting her to piss at all.
SGANARELLE	What! A fine thing! Make her piss lots! Lots! If every invalid pissed like this, I'd gladly be a doctor for the rest of my life.

For the rest of his life Molière, though his genius led him in other directions, never completely abandoned this kind of play. This was what had won him his theatre in Paris, and continued to provide some box-office security. As the account books show, whenever a more ambitious venture had failed, or business was bad for any reason, Molière could usually recoup his losses by turning out another Italian farce. Though the critics might sneer, he knew what the public would pay good money to see. Let us examine one such potboiler in greater detail: *Les Fourberies de Scapin*, (*Scapin and his Tricks*) a late work, written in 1671, and one of the best known.

Several of Molière's plays had specific classical models. His *Amphitryon* was taken from Plautus' comedy of the same name. *L'Avare* (*The Miser*) was based on the same author's *The Pot of Gold*. *Les Fourberies de Scapin* derives from Terence's *Phormio*, one of the standard Roman plots about two sons who have taken advantage of their fathers' absences to become involved with two apparently unsuitable young women. Phormio, a seedy acquaintance, who makes his living by his wits, takes on the task of duping the fathers into accepting these misalliances. The plot, then, is Roman. So is a good deal of the dialogue. Here is a speech in which the servant Scapin attempts to console one of the fathers for life's misfortunes:

Whenever the head of the household goes away, be it for never so short a time, he ought to make a mental inventory of all the upsets he might expect to find on his return – his house burned down, his money stolen, his wife dead, his son a cripple, his daughter seduced. And whatever he finds hasn't happened, he should credit to good fortune. I always practice this in my own humble philosophy, and I've never come back home without expecting a furious master, reprimands, insults, cuts, kicks and lashings, and whatever I escaped, I thanked my lucky stars for it.

This is not adaptation but translation; the speech comes almost verbatim from Terence.

On to this skeleton, however, Molière grafts the more vivid and immediate characters of the *commedia*. In this too he was probably not original. He seems to have borrowed from an earlier version of the story, *Le Pédant Joué* (*The Pedant Tricked*) by Cyrano de Bergerac, reputedly his old schoolfellow. The age had no law of copyright, and it is pointless to talk of plagiarism. Like all his contemporaries, Molière both sinned and was sinned against. His version, in any case, is far livelier than Cyrano's. The characters are all drawn from stock, but depicted with considerable individuality. Octave and Leandre, the two young men in trouble, are the standard lovers of the Italian comedies, but of markedly different natures. Octave is sentimental, inert, tearfully resigned to his fate. Here he describes how he first met his beloved, in a house of mourning:

OCTAVE   Curiosity made me urge Leandre to investigate. We entered a room, and there saw an old lady on her deathbed, with a servant woman weeping and wailing over her; and a girl, dissolved in tears, the most beautiful, the most heart-rending sight you ever saw.

SCAPIN   Aha!

OCTAVE   Anyone else in her condition would have looked a wreck. She was wearing nothing but a cheap shirt with a plain cambric nightdress over it, and a yellow cap pushed high on her head which let her hair tumble loose around her shoulders. And yet, even like this, she was infinitely alluring, every inch of her exquisitely adorable.

In a rash moment, Octave married the girl. Now he is terrified of what will happen when his father finds out. Leandre, by contrast, is more fiery and impetuous. He has fallen madly in love with a young gypsy, and is at his wit's end to find money to buy her from her tribe.

Quick to sense a slight and pick a quarrel, he turns his resentment on Scapin, whom he suspects of betraying him:

> No, Octave, I'll have him make a clean breast of his duplicity here and now. Yes, you snake-in-the-grass! The game's up! I know all about it! You probably thought they wouldn't let it out. But I'll have a confession from your own lips, or I'll run you through with my sword!

It takes the pressing sense of his own need to calm him down, and make him realise how much he and Octave depend on Scapin's wits to relieve their predicament.

Their servants are similarly matched. Sylvestre, Octave's man, is lugubrious and resigned, the more stolid type of the Italian clown and only dragged into villainy against his will. Scapin, the master-mind, both gives his name to the play and takes it directly from Italian sources: Scapino was one of the more resourceful and inventive *commedia* servants, and Molière's character takes the same delight in outwitting authority:

> As a matter of fact, there's not much I can't do when I set my mind to it. Yes, I have been blessed with a certain talent. I'm a master of polite prevarication, of intricate intrigue – or, to use the vulgar misnomer, swindles. I can say in all modesty that there has never existed a more expert practitioner of subterfuge, or one who has acquired greater distinction in that honourable profession. But, God knows, merit's at a discount nowadays. I was involved in something which had rather disagreeable consequences, and went straight into retirement.

Molière played Scapin himself, and the brush with the law here alluded to may be an autobiographical comment by a playwright whose irreverence often landed him in trouble; like his character, Molière was no respecter of persons. Certainly the role was tailor-made for the actor-playwright. Scapin dominates the play. He is the puppet-master who makes the others dance. This effect was beautifully suggested in Jean-Louis Barrault's production, where Scapin made his first appearance over a high wall, looking down at the lesser beings whose destinies he would control. In addition, Scapin is himself an actor. His part calls for a series of impersonations and chameleon-like adaptations to changing circumstances; it needs an equally fine actor to bring it to life.

The Pantalone of this play is Géronte, Leandre's father and Scapin's master, censorious and avaricious. Argante, Octave's father, is more pompous and orotund, with a good deal of the *Dottore* in him. Finally, the two girls: Hyacinthe, the negligible *ingénue* role, and the gypsy Zerbinette (Terence's flute-girl brought up to date), a more vigorous soubrette part adapted to the talents of Mlle Beauval, who had a strident and infectious stage laugh.

The plot, as we have said, is basically Terence's. Octave dreads the consequences of his hasty marriage with Hyacinthe, the damsel in distress, while Leandre needs money to buy his gypsy's freedom. Scapin takes their affairs in hand, devising a series of ruses both to stave off the parental wrath and find money to assist the boys' urgent need. Both fathers have to be duped. Argante is determined to have the marriage annulled in court. Scapin tries to scare him off by demonstrating the perils of the legal system:

Oh sir, what a thing to say! What an idea! Cast your eyes over the devious ways of justice; consider the numbers of appeals, the constant move from court to court, the never-ending hearings, the publicity; the long line of bloodsuckers with claws outstretched – bailiffs, lawyers, counsellors, registrars, substitutes, reporters, judges and their clerks. There's not one among the lot of them who isn't capable of abusing the best law in the world on the most trivial pretext. The bailiff will issue a forged writ, on which you'll be condemned before you know where you are. Your lawyer will enter into collusion with your opponent, and sell you for hard cash. Your counsellor will yield to the same temptation, and either vanish when the case comes up, or else talk in circles and never get to the point. The registrar will issue an injunction against you by default. The reporter's clerk will mislay documents, or the reporter will misquote them. And when, after taking every imaginable precaution, you've managed to get through all this unscathed, you'll be aghast to discover that the judges have been prejudiced against you, either by the bigots, or by their own mistresses. Oh sir, keep clear of that inferno at all costs. It's hell on earth to have to go to law. The very thought of a lawsuit is enough to send me packing to the Indies.

When this does not work, Sylvestre is brought in to masquerade as Hyacinthe's ruffianly brother, in an impersonation recalling the Spanish Captain of the *commedia*:

SYLVESTRE   Death, blood and guts! If I find that man I'll have his hide, if they put me on the rack for it!

SCAPIN   Sir, Octave's father is no coward. You may not frighten him one little bit.

SYLVESTRE   Oh, won't I! Hell's teeth! If I had him here now I'd give him a taste of steel in his belly!

Argante, terrorised into submission, hands over the money. Géronte, in his turn, is told an elaborate fiction of his son's kidnapping by Turkish pirates; whining, weeping, expostulating, he finally hands over the ransom money. But Géronte must suffer further punishment. In a scene which is pure *commedia*, Scapin persuades him that he is being hunted by a gang of ruffians. To escape, Géronte hides in a sack where, unable to see, he is repeatedly thrashed by Scapin masquerading as a series of people with different voices and accents.

This kind of comedy is anarchic in that it subvents the customary patterns of society. Parental authority is flouted, the rights of personal property are endangered, lies triumph over truth, and general licence prevails. Molière, however, tempers this anarchy with a reassurance of bourgeois values. The two girls are no mere lights-of-love, but have a realistic concern for the material advantages of marriage.

SCAPIN   What my master's just done for you should give you heart to respond to his passion with your own.

ZERBINETTE   I don't yet trust him completely, and what he's done still doesn't make me entirely sure. I have a merry nature, and laugh at everything; but under the laughter there are still some things that I take seriously. Your master is mistaken if he thinks that just because he bought me I'm his body and soul. That will cost him something more than money. If I'm to respond to his love as he hopes, I need a pledge of his good faith, served up with certain conventional ceremonies.

And, at the end of the play, we are reassured that the aberrations have been only temporary. Society is affirmed. Scapin is discovered, begs for pardon, and is generously forgiven. The two girls turn out to be eminently suitable after all. Hyacinthe is identified as Géronte's daughter, believed to have been lost at sea. Zerbinette is revealed as Argante's daughter, kidnapped by gypsies when she was four years old. The obligatory happy ending is also an assurance to the audience of values so firmly rooted that one may joke about them with impunity, for nothing can ever shake them.

Les Fourberies de Scapin is thus a frothy concoction, put together from several sources and mixed by a skilled hand, whose prime intent is to please. Even so slight a piece, however, reveals certain fundamental attitudes and patterns which carry over into Molière's more serious work. Although, in his longer plays, he may appear to discard the outward forms of the *commedia*, some of its values remain implicit in everything he writes. Most obviously, he continues to exploit, refine and develop certain types of *commedia* character. The *Dottore* continues to reappear throughout his work in one particular aspect, the quack Doctor of Medicine who passes superstition off as science, and cloaks ignorance in Latin. Critics of the biographical school suggest that this shows Molière's preoccupation with his own ill-health; there is certainly a marked incidence of 'doctor' plays in his later years. Certainly, too, the contemporary state of the profession left it wide open to ridicule; some of the pronouncements made in all seriousness by doctors of the time are more fantastic than anything Molière could have invented, and the medical student's qualifying examination was a farce in itself. Molière's obsession with doctors, however, probably goes deeper than these explanations would suggest. It stems from a particular view of human nature which is nourished by his theatrical environment and informs his concept of comedy.

Molière owed a great deal to the Italians; and in the *commedia dell' arte*, a character's principal attribute was his mask. This served both to label the character and provide him with a constant frame of reference. Each of the major *commedia* figures has his characteristic foibles and mode of expression which remain the same throughout the action. They do not modulate. They neither undergo subtle character changes themselves, nor work such changes upon others. Change, when it occurs at all, tends to be arbitrary and abrupt, as if a character had taken off one mask and replaced it with another. The soul of the character is in the mask, and the mask is in the soul. Although, on Molière's stage, the mask had largely disappeared as a physical adjunct to the performance, the habits inspired by the mask persisted. Molière's characters still wear their masks, but spiritually. They continue to embody distinct types of human folly; they try to enforce their prejudices on others, and wear their affectations like blinkers. In psychological terms, the mask is translated into an obsession, which may be revealed to the audience by significant repetitions of language and behaviour. In Les Fourberies de Scapin, Géronte, though maskless, is an example of a man obsessed. His thought is only for his money; it has eradicated almost all traces of human feeling from him. Thus we have the bitter-comic scene in which the miser learns of his son's supposed kidnapping; the money-machine rediscovers a vestigial paternal instinct.

GERONTE	Go tell that Turk to send me back my son, and put yourself in his place till I've got the ransom money together.
SCAPIN	Do you know what you're saying? Do you think this Turk is so stupid he'll take a nobody like me in place of your son?
GERONTE	What the devil was he doing on that galley?
SCAPIN	He had no idea that things would turn out so badly. Don't forget, he's only given me two hours!
GERONTE	You say he asks—
SCAPIN	Five hundred crowns.
GERONTE	Five hundred crowns! Has he no conscience?
SCAPIN	Of course. The conscience of a Turk.
GERONTE	Does he know what five hundred crowns are?
SCAPIN	Yes. Fifteen hundred pounds.
GERONTE	Does he think you can sweep up fifteen hundred pounds in the gutter?
SCAPIN	Unreasonable people, Turks.
GERONTE	But what the devil was he doing on that galley?
SCAPIN	True. But we don't have second sight, do we? For pity's sake stop wasting time.
GERONTE	Here. This is the key to my closet.
SCAPIN	Good.
GERONTE	Open it—
SCAPIN	With pleasure.
GERONTE	You'll find a large key on the left hand side. The key to my attic.
SCAPIN	Right.
GERONTE	Take all the old clothes you find in the big hamper. Sell them to the junk shop, and go and buy back my son.
SCAPIN	Are you dreaming? I shouldn't get a hundred francs for the lot. Besides, you know how little time I have.
GERONTE	But what the devil was he doing in that galley?

This is the kind of characterisation that Molière developed in the plays for Paris audiences that he began to write immediately after returning to the capital. In his class-conscious society he found many examples of the 'mask', in real life no less than on the stage. His first Paris play, *Les Précieuses Ridicules* (*The Affected Young Ladies*) deals with the mask of social affectation, consciously assumed to impress one's associates. The young ladies of the title have constructed for themselves an artificial world which professes to repudiate the vulgar and common-place. But their masks so hamper their vision that they can no longer distinguish between reality and pretence in others: they are easily deceived by two servants masquerading as gentlemen. In the quack doctors of several comedies, we see the mask of spurious learning assumed for profit. Molière's most notorious play, *Tartuffe*, shows the mask of religious hypocrisy worn by a spiritual adviser in a wealthy household. While affecting the highest Christian principles, he is secretly robbing his patron and attempting to seduce his wife.

Alternatively, there is the other kind of mask, less consciously assumed but still potent: the mask of habit, of social convenience, worn so long and become so familiar that it warps and diminishes the human being beneath. In *L'Ecole des Femmes* (*The School for Wives*) Arnolphe is obsessed with the idea of raising a girl to be the perfect wife; kept in ignorance of other men, she will never learn to be unfaithful. Arnolphe's comic tragedy is that his fixation blinds him to the very evils he is trying to avoid. He sees only what he wants to see, so that his ward finds it easy to obey her nature and escape with the young man she really loves. Orgon, the wealthy bourgeois in *Tartuffe*, is similarly obsessed with the externals of religious devotion. Though evidence is brought repeatedly before his eyes, he can see no evil in Tartuffe. Often these obsessions are revealed in language. Géronte, driven to desperation, can only cry 'What the devil was he doing on that galley?' Orgon's only response to domestic news is a reiterated 'And Tartuffe?' M. Jourdain in *Le Bourgeois Gentilhomme* asks of every new scheme patently designed to defraud him, 'Is this what people of quality do?'

Les Fourberies de Scapin deals, on a superficial level, with a world temporarily out of joint, and shows how order and social propriety are eventually restored. The more serious comedies pursue the same theme with greater depth and intensity. They show a way of life malformed by some aberration or obsession which has to be cured, sometimes by violent means, before a more rational and ordered existence can resume. The aberration, while it provokes laughter, may be positively dangerous in that it threatens health and safety, or the well being of family and property. Molière's common practice is to plant in the play some dispassionate observer, the *raisonneur*, who points the way that the aberrant character should go, and opposes his calm common-sense to the folly of vanity and excess. Yet the fixation is usually so far gone that a cure is out of the *raisonneur's* hands; it must be brought about by external circumstances, or by the fact that the delusion precipitates its own crisis, bringing the character irrevocably, unmistakeably, face to face with the consequences of his own folly. Thus Molière's comedies become deeply felt statements about the human condition.

To see this more insightful Molière, as well as other aspects of his complex art, we may turn to another of the later plays, *Le Bourgeois Gentilhomme* (*The Self-made Gentleman*). This appeared a year before *Les Fourberies de Scapin*; it was created for a royal command performance in October 1670, and put into the commercial repertory a month later. It is a compendium of Molière's career, revealing the showman as well as the psychologist, the entertainer and the observer of his times. Written, supposedly, to commemorate a trivial occasion, it has won an enduring place in the repertory. Louis and his court are said to have found it unamusing at first representation. Even if the story is true – it probably is not – the royal verdict has been triumphantly reversed by the centuries. *Le Bourgeois Gentilhomme* has been more frequently revived, and more consistently popular, than anything else Molière wrote.

Another story, more firmly founded, claims that the work began as a *pièce d' occasion*. At the end of the previous year a Turkish embassy had visited Paris. We seem them, turbanned, in a contemporary picture, presenting themselves before the King. They failed to endear themselves. In French eyes, they lacked the social graces; their turbans were dirty, and they seemed indifferent to the marks of favour bestowed upon them. It was suggested to Molière, through Finance Minister Colbert, that he might avenge the ruffled dignity of the monarch through a *comédie-ballet* burlesquing Turkish manners and customs. Assuming the story to be true, we thus have a play written backwards, for the Turkish ballet does not appear until Act Four. At best, *Le Bourgeois Gentilhomme* could only have been a half-hearted act of revenge, for the Turkish embassy had already left court by the time the play opened. Perhaps we may attribute the Turkish element at least as much to the perennial fascination with Turkish affairs that we have already seen so strongly marked in tragedy, and which appears even in such little ways as the fictional Turkish pirates in *Les Fourberies de Scapin*.

The Turks, then, were not offended, for they had already gone home.

It appears that no one else was particularly offended either, and that Molière, for once in his life, had picked a safe subject. He needed one. After so many plays which had provoked varying degrees of resentment, a comedy which upset no one must have seemed highly desirable. Although several particular models have been suggested for M. Jourdain, the *nouveau riche* of the title, no one seems to have complained at the time. Presented with a play about a *bourgeois* who seeks to rise above his station, the *bourgeoisie* could not be offended, for it found such pretensions ridiculous. Nor could the aristocracy be offended, for its entrenched position was unassailable. A gentleman was born, not made (though Lully, and a few others, proved the contrary); the Jourdains of this world were pygmies struggling against divine dispensation. We shall suggest later that there is some social criticism in the piece, but it passed its immediate audience by. This seems to be borne out by a charming little play that appeared at the Hôtel de Bourgogne in 1674, the year after Molière's death. Called *L'Ombre de Molière* (*The Shade of Molière*) it is a posthumous tribute to the playwright through the words of his major characters. Molière is represented as standing trial in the Underworld – a classical Underworld, presided over by the Greek Judges of the Dead. To decide his place among the ghosts, they confront him with a series of accusers, the principal targets of his plays. A *précieuse* is there, claiming that her language and life-style have been ridiculed. A *petit marquis*, one of Molière's familiar butts, registers his complaint. The doctors, of course, appear in force. 'I knew there must be a lot of doctors up there,' remarks the judge, 'because there are so many dead down here.' There are also characters from *Le Bourgeois Gentilhomme*, but not M. Jourdain, as one might expect. Mme Jourdain is there, simply to exploit some of the tricks of phrase that Molière had given her, and Nicole, the maid, is chosen for her infectious laugh. She at least has no complaints. When asked what she has to say against the accused, she replies 'He's a good ghost. And believe me, M. Pluto, he's the best item in your bag.' *Le Bourgeois Gentilhomme*, then, seems to have been remembered for the rich individuality of its characters, rather than for its satire, and this has been the key to its popularity ever since.

The play traditionally stemmed from the ballet, and it is ballet form that dictates its structure. It is *comèdie-ballet* by definition; its high point is the Turkish ballet of Act Four; and it ends with another ballet commissioned for M. Jourdain's entertainment as part of the action. In the court presentation, both Lully and Beauchamp danced in it, and Lully wrote the music, which still survives. In addition to these formal dance sequences, ballet elements appear throughout the work. The action unfolds in an unbroken sequence, the pattern of ballet rather than of drama proper. Dances evolving from the action, in the manner of *Les Fâcheux*, provide the links between the acts. Acts One and Two, both brief, are little more than a series of *entrées* and *divertissements*, representing the various arts and professions contributing to M. Jourdain's gentlemanly education. Act One shows him with his music and dancing masters. A song is offered, and he replies with one of his own. There follows a *dialogue en musique*, parodying the fashionable pastoral mode:

MUSIC MASTER	Forward, please. [*The performers enter*]. As you see, they are dressed as shepherds.
M. JOURDAIN	Why does it have to be shepherds all the time? Everywhere I look, there's shepherds!
DANCING MASTER	Whenever one wants to make people converse in music, one puts them into a pastoral setting. That is realism. From time immemorial shepherds have sung to each other. It would hardly be natural to have a musical dialogue between princes or tradesmen.

The act closes with a ballet interlude in the form of a dancing lesson, in which 'four dancers execute the whole range of movements and every variety of step, to the Dancing Master's orders.'

Act Two brings a Fencing Master and a Professor of Philosophy, followed by the Tailor with four apprentices who 'perform a dance of gratitude for M. Jourdain's generosity.' In Act Three Jourdain, ridiculed by his family, arranges a banquet for a titled lady he is hoping to seduce: 'Six cooks, who have prepared the feast, dance together for the third *intermède*, finally bringing in a table set with several dishes.' Act Four has the Turkish ballet, and Act Five concludes with the entertainment commissioned by Jourdain for his guests, a self-contained work which is the most elaborate spectacle of all.

Within this framework, the scenes are balanced with precision. Though this is a prose comedy, it is structured as mathematically as a Racinian verse tragedy. We see M. Jourdain's folly growing until, in the middle of Act Three, he is prepared to sacrifice wife and family to gratify his whims. He plots to take an aristocratic mistress; he denies his daughter the man she loves, so that she may marry a marquis. In the great scene of the family conference, all this comes to a head.

Jourdain's power, as master of the household, is real. However much his wife and daughter may protest, his word is law. From this midpoint, the play charts his downfall. The domestic tyrant is deceived by all about him, so that by the end of the play, none of his ambitions has been accomplished; though he continues to live in his fool's paradise, the rest of the world has resumed its serene and orderly course. Individual scenes display the same internal symmetry, particularly the *pas de quatre* of the love scenes. Molière gives us two pairs of lovers. Lucile, Jourdain's daughter, is wooed by Cléonte, while his servant Covielle pursues Lucile's maid Nicole. In a scene of quadruple misunderstanding, one pair echoes the other:

LUCILE	There's a lot of fuss about nothing! Cleonte, let me tell you exactly why I pretended not to see you this morning.
NICOLE	And I'd like to tell you what made us go by in such a hurry.
COVIELLE	I don't want to listen to a word.
LUCILE	Listen! This morning . . .
CLEONTE	No, I tell you!
NICOLE	Let me tell you!
COVIELLE	Deceiver! No!
LUCILE	Just hear what I have to say!
CLEONTE	I'm not interested.
NICOLE	Let me speak!
COVIELLE	I've gone deaf.
LUCILE	Cleonte!
CLEONTE	No!
NICOLE	Covielle!
COVIELLE	I won't!

Then the pattern is reversed, with the young men pleading and the girls refusing to listen. Here comic prose displays the same formality of structure as tragic verse.

The same kind of balance is seen in the play's theme. Molière is writing of the two kinds of life-style coexisting in his society, the bourgeois and the aristocratic, each with its own set of values. The humour arises when two systems normally distinct are brought into juxtaposition. There are, perhaps, two sorts of parody. One works by exaggeration, selecting certain aspects of the subject and distorting them to the point where they become ridiculous. This Molière does not really do. Most of his scenes are based on accurate observation of contemporary behaviour. His Music and Dancing Masters, as we have seen, are full of their own subjects, but what they say about music and dance is orthodox contemporary theory. The speech lesson administered to Jourdain by the Professor of Philosophy is hilariously funny in context, but may be found almost word for word in a textbook of the period. Molière finds humour in more subtle ways, by the parody of contrast. Set a philosopher beside an illiterate, and both appear ridiculous. Match a tradesman with an aristocrat, and ways of life which are poles apart draw humour from each other by comparison.

On the psychological level, M. Jourdain is a prime example of Molière's 'obsessed' characters. His fixation is with the ideal of gentility. To secure this end, he is prepared to sacrifice money, dignity, even his own family. All the virtues of his former life have been discarded, sacrificed on the altar of social ambition. The man who was shrewd enough to amass a fortune is now so overwhelmed by the glamour of nobility that he is prepared to lend money to any shady acquaintance with a title. Occasionally we see a momentary reawakening of financial caution, a relic of the old Jourdain, but this is all too easily overcome; he can be persuaded to take useless lessons or buy a shoddy suit because 'this is what the gentry do.' His humble parentage must be denied, to be replaced by any agreeable fiction. His daughter must marry a marquis. Thus what began as a foible, an eccentricity, has become a disease which threatens the solidarity of his family; the man who has lost sight of his proper place in the scheme of things becomes a threat to social order.

In the face of this dementia, his wife functions as an unavailing *raissoneuse*:

That's a thing I'll never give my consent to. When you marry above your station, you're no longer your own mistress. Your life becomes unbearable. I don't want any man for a son-in-law who can throw my daughter's parents in her face. I don't want her to have children who'll be ashamed to call me granny. Suppose she comes to call on me, all high and mighty in her carriage and pair, and accidentally goes past someone in the neighbourhood without recognizing them or saying good morning? Oh, their tongues would start wagging fast enough then. 'See the great lady, putting on airs! M. Jourdain's daughter, that is! We were good enough for her when she was little. She wasn't always as grand as she is now. Her father's father kept a draper's shop. Her mother's father, too. They made a pile for their children – and they may be paying for it dearly now, in the other world! Nobody ever got that rich by being honest!' That's the kind of cackle I can do without. I want a man, to put it in one word, who thinks it's a privilege to marry my daughter. A man to whom I can say 'Sit yourself down, son-in-law, and take pot luck!'

For Molière, pretentiousness is always ridiculous. Even the honest Cléonte does not entirely escape. His romantic ardours are deflated by the earthy practicality of his servant:

CLEONTE	After all my burning sighs, the lover's vows I paid as tribute to her charms ...
COVIELLE	After all those hours I spent paying court to her, all the little services and attentions in the kitchen ...
CLEONTE	All the tears I shed at her feet ...
COVIELLE	All the buckets of water I drew from the well for her ...
CLEONTE	All the burning passion I displayed, cherishing her above my own self ...
COVIELLE	All the burning heat I had to suffer, when I took her place to turn the roast ...

But M. Jourdain is too far gone to listen to the voice of reason. For the sake of the family and society, this baneful influence must be exorcised. A desperate cure is effected, not by forcing the invalid to acknowledge the disease, but by allowing him to persist in it to the point where he is completely out of touch with reality. This is the function of the Turkish ballet. M. Jourdain is informed that the son of the Grand Turk wishes to marry his daughter, and that he himself is to be elevated to the highest rank of the Turkish nobility. The Turks, of course, are only actors, and the suitor is Cléonte in disguise. The ballet-ceremony is a preposterous farce, patent to everyone except Jourdain. Its language is a farrago of Turkish, Arabic, lingua franca and gibberish. Some of it Molière stole unashamedly from another Turkish play. Some of it is highly obscene, a fact usually tactfully ignored by editors and translators. Jourdain swallows it whole; and thus the Turkish ballet, apart from satisfying the whim of Louis XIV and Colbert, performs an important dramatic function. It is a visual realisation of Jourdain's mental state: a fantasy world, in which appearance masquerades as truth. Jourdain emerges as a Don Quixote, happy in a world that his own imagination has created.

Is there any social criticism in this play? Perhaps; but it is delicately hinted at, and never obtrusive. With the exception of M. Jourdain, the *bourgeoisie* comes off well. Molière puts into the mouth of Cléonte a stirring defence of bourgeois virtues:

> The word 'gentleman' is small change nowadays. People lay claim to the title without scruple; and the common practice seems to be to make it the property of anyone who cares to take it. For my own part, I have somewhat more delicate feelings on the subject. I believe that an honest man should never pretend to be something he is not. I believe that if a man attempts to disguise the birthright that was bestowed on him by heaven; if he parades before the world in a borrowed title; if he wishes to pass himself off for something other than what he is; then that man, sir, is a scoundrel. I can say with confidence that I was born to respectable parents; that I have done my military service – six years, sir, with honourable discharge; and that I consider myself sufficiently qualified to maintain an adequate position in the world. But in spite of all that, I am not willing to give myself a name that other men in my position might believe they could lay claim to. And I will tell you, quite frankly, that no, sir, I am not a gentleman.

The aristocracy does not come off nearly so well. We are made aware of the difference between M. Jourdain's dream of the nobility and the reality. For him, the upper classes have no blemish. He can only grow by association with them:

> Does it bring me anything but honour, to have a person of this quality seen visiting my house so often, calling me his dear friend, treating me like an equal? He has done me favours you couldn't even begin to guess. And right in front of everybody, he put his arm around me, laid his hand on my shoulder – it struck me all of a heap!

But for the world of high society in which he wishes to move, M. Jourdain's sole attraction is his money. This is unequivocally stated by the Music Master at the beginning of the play:

> Let's be honest. Here's a man of small enlightenment, who never knows the right things to say, and always applauds at the wrong moments. But what he lacks in culture he makes up in money. His purse knows what's good, even if he doesn't, and his kind of praise you can take to the bank.

Fair enough; the professional entertainer states Molière's own position. But the same money-grubbing attitude is displayed by the aristocrats themselves. We see two of them in the play. One is Dorante, a shabby count who uses Jourdain's money to feather his own nest. Most of it goes to buy presents for the rich widow he is pursuing; nor is he ashamed to pretend to act as Jourdain's go-between in making assignations with the same widow. Arrogant and condescending to Jourdain's face, he barely bothers to keep up the pretence of flattery; behind his back, he is openly abusive.

Dorimène, the widow, though less actively involved, is little better. Both she and Dorante are so secure in the privileges of birth that they look upon the upstart as fair game. Such honour as they still possess is reserved for their own kind. They have no sense of humanity or fair dealing. This is the true face of the world that Jourdain seeks to enter. We have no indication that Molière's courtly audience was incensed by this, or that they interpreted these characters as in any sense a criticism of their own class. The privilege of rank conferred its own immunity. But the criticism is apparent, none the less; and while it would be absurd to call *Le Bourgeois Gentilhomme* a revolutionary work, it indicates the way the wind was blowing; it looks forward to plays more obviously critical of the class-structure, which would appear in greater numbers in the eighteenth century; and it anticipates, ever so faintly, the dissatisfaction with inherited rank and privilege that would reach its catastrophic culmination in the Revolution.

8 Survivals

It was Molière's final disappointment, in a life that had been full of them, that he did not die to a full house. We can imagine him, money-cautious as he always was, running his eyes over the empty seats as he struggled through the agonies of his last performance of *Le Malade Imaginaire*. The *parterre* was a little fuller than it had been the last time they played – the cheap tickets usually sold well – but the *loges* were down, less than half the previous receipts. Such was the fickleness of the Paris public, even with regard to new plays. An opening would always pack the house, but after the first two or three nights the crowds would dwindle until the next novelty sparked their interest. Given these imperatives of the actor's life, there was little time for sentiment. In his account-book Hubert inserted a brief, business-like note: 'No performances Sunday or Tuesday, because of the death of M. de Molière on (Feb) 17th at 10 p.m.' Three days after their leader's furtive, shameful funeral, the Palais Royal reopened with *Le Misanthrope*. This had never been a popular play, and the takings dropped again. In March, *Le Malade Imaginaire* returned to the repertory, with La Thorillière taking over the role that Molière had written for himself. Receipts rose spectacularly; probably the play now had a ghoulish curiosity value, and there must have been a good deal of interest in how the company would manage without its guiding spirit. They were even greater on 5 March, when Monsieur, the King's brother, and his wife attended the theatre in person. *Le Malade Imaginaire* continued to be played, but the takings soon fell off again, and there was now no Molière to revitalise the company, or dash off a new popular hit.

La Grange and Armande took over the direction, but could not fill the gap. In the eternal rivalry of the theatres, the Hôtel de Bourgogne seized this propitious opportunity to conduct a raid. La Thorillière, the Beauvals man and wife – she of the famous laugh – and the brilliant Baron, still only twenty, went over to the older house. Thus weakened, the company found itself unable to reopen after the Easter recess, and at the end of April the theatre was given to the insistent Lully. The Palais Royal, however, was not alone in its difficulties. Since the Marais had also been closed down by royal command, the remnants of the troupes amalgamated as the Troupe du Roi at the Hôtel de Guénégaud. They played safe by opening their new theatre, across the river on the Left Bank, with *Tartuffe*, still, and for a long time to come, a box office winner. For a while Molière's plays formed the whole repertory, though a few machine plays, using the old equipment of the Marais, were later added.

In 1674, Brécourt brought out *L' Ombre de Molière* at the Hôtel de Bourgogne. Obviously, Molière's death had done much to appease his old enemies. Brécourt dedicated his play to the Duc d' Enghien, who some years earlier had been similarly honoured by Boursault's *Le Portrait du Peintre* (*The Painter Painted*), a vicious attack on Molière. So much had the mood changed that Brécourt was now able to write: 'Merely permit, Monseigneur, that the works of Molière may hold some place in your library, and that my comedy may serve as a kind of index to his.' His play was a sincere tribute. We have already seen its nature; it is a retrospective exhibition of favourite themes and jokes, a reprise of some of Molière's most popular characters. We are given a capsule summary of Molière's career:

> There used to be a man up there who dabbled in writing, so I'm told; but he made himself so hard to please that he found some imperfection in everything. He started by criticising particular fashions of speech. Then he went on to clothes; then he attacked people's characters, and inconsiderately set out to find fault with all the follies of the world. He could never bring himself to put up with any of the long train of abuses that he saw there. He stripped the veil from every mystery, publicly exposed the self-interest that motivated mankind, and did it so well that, because of the new light he shed on these things, just about every aspect of human existence started to have a bit of a comic side.

The comedy ends with the Judge of the Dead awarding Molière a place among the immortals: 'Now it is time for me to name the place your shade and memory will occupy. It must be for posterity to find a place for you; and while it labours for your greater glory, take your seat between Plautus and Terence.' Thus Molière is placed between the two great comic writers of the Roman world, whose plays he had often used as the basis for his own.

Though Molière's work provided a firm base for the combined companies, they now felt strong enough to challenge the Hôtel de Bourgogne in its own domain of tragedy. For a while, Bourgogne and Guénégaud were in cut-throat competition. When the Bourgogne presented Racine's *Iphigenie*, the Guénégaud countered with a rival version. When the older house staged *Phèdre*, the younger opened Pradon's play a few days later; and Pradon was judged the more immediately successful. In 1679 the traffic began to flow the other way, when the actress La Champmeslé crossed to the Guénégaud and brought the Racine repertory with her. But the Guénégaud was still plagued with financial troubles, Louis XIV's interest in the theatre was at a low ebb and, as part of his centralisation policy, the rival theatres were fused into one in 1680. Some marks of royal favour continued. The new company – now the Comedie Française – inherited the Bourgogne's annual subsidy. Though La Grange remained as administrator, the wife of the Dauphin assumed general control. Thus the actors acquired a measure of security at the cost of some of their earlier privileges. Distribution of roles was now likely to be imposed on them from above, and, as an office of the court, the theatre began to suffer from a bureaucratic fussiness which has never completely disappeared.

A continuing problem was to find a new theatre. In 1687 the company was planning to open at the College des Quatre Nations, built out of Cardinal Mazarin's fortune after his death. There was loud clerical opposition, and the king, his mind elsewhere, was unwilling to lend his authority to the players' side. Perhaps he thought he had already antagonised the church enough for Molière's sake. A second choice fell victim to the same protests, then a third. It was the old story; a theatre might be tolerable in the abstract, but not in bricks and mortar in one's own parish. Finally the company settled on a *jeu-de-paume* in Saint-Germain-des-Près. As the Hotel de Guénégaud had been located in the same parish, clerical objections could not logically apply, and the tennis-court, remodelled and rechristened the Theatre Royal, became the company's home from 1689 to 1770. It was built on an elliptical plan, in the Italian style, and opened with La Champmeslé in *Phèdre*, accompanied by a Molière farce.

In all these negotiations, the moving spirit was La Grange. Molière's administrative duties had devolved upon him, and he discharged them with grace and skill. In the organisation of the united company, it was he who functioned as the actors' representative at court; it was he who led the search for new quarters; he continued to serve as accountant; and in 1682, he performed for Molière the service that Heminges and

Condell had done for Shakespeare, by bringing out the first complete, corrected edition of his works, collated from manuscripts which have long since disappeared. He also advanced as an actor. In his early career, we saw him playing mostly lover's roles. By the time of his death, in 1692, he was playing some of the major roles in the canon: Tartuffe, Alceste, M. Jourdain. He was fifty-three when he died, and the pressures of the theatre were with him, as with Molière, to the last; in the final month of his life he had acted twenty-two times, and only surrendered the company treasury a few days before his death. With his passing, another link with the old regime was broken. Molière's family line quickly returned to middle-class obscurity. Armande remarried, but produced no illustrious progeny.

For a time, it seemed that Molière's brain children would be subjected to the same fate. For a good part of the eighteenth century, he suffered the inevitable eclipse that falls upon great writers for a generation or two after their deaths. Just as Shakespeare, in England, could only be tolerated in an adapted form, so Molière's comedies were permitted to remain in the repertory on sufferance, as an act of piety. In 1739 Voltaire could write 'The theatre is empty when these comedies are played . . . hardly anyone goes to *Tartuffe* any more – the same play that, in the old days, drew all Paris.' Although much of his theatrical legacy had passed to others, his own works were now considered a little crude and old-fashioned. The mood of audiences, and of the times, had changed. A different social pattern was forming, in which the inherited privileges of the aristocracy were being eroded away by new wealth. A more assertive bourgeois audience filled the theatre, demanding attention to its tastes and standards, which were inclined towards the genteel and sentimental.

For the new kind of French dramatist, we may look at the only one who was really entitled to call himself Molière's successor, Marivaux. He had inherited his predecessor's sharpness of phrasing and depiction; he had inherited, too, the mechanics and characters of the *commedia dell' arte*, though these had been purged of their grossness and given a more sophisticated air. Marivaux's Arlequin is the descendant of the Italian Arlecchino, but at several generations' remove. His manners have improved, and he can be taken into polite society without offending anybody. 'Silver comedy' tends to exhibit the same characteristics across the centuries, and Marivaux's is for the most part no exception. It is elegant, pretty, short on plot and social commentary, but strong in sentimentality. Its action springs mostly from affairs of the heart, whose ramifications are explored in affectionate, sensitive detail. It tends to favour a romanticised pastoral setting, which has little contact with the harsh actuality of the countryside. In 1670, M. Jourdain was already complaining of the ubiquity of shepherds in the arts. With Marivaux, we are moving rapidly towards the time of Marie Antoinette, playing at being a shepherdess in the perfumed tranquillity of Le Petit Trianon. The English, passing through a similar phase in their own theatre, talked much of 'sensibility', or, as we should now say, sentimentality. In France, the favoured form of comedy was *comédie larmoyante*, comedy with tears.

One play by Marivaux, blunter than most, deserves particular attention as an index of its times. This is *Le Triomphe de Plutus* (*The Triumph of Plutus*) which frames a serious social statement in a celestial metaphor. The short comedy concerns a duel of wits between two gods, to see which is the more powerful. Apollo is god of the arts, who shows his power in poetry and music. Plutus (who had, centuries earlier, lent his name to a comedy by Aristophanes) is the god of wealth. Coarse, blunt and sensual, he still wields the omnipotent weapon of hard cash. Their dispute arises over a mortal girl whom Apollo is courting. Plutus, to demonstrate his superiority, lays siege to the house with his wealth. The girl's maid is easily suborned by the presents offered by this strange visitor who calls himself M. Richard – as he points out, the stress is on the first syllable. The girl's uncle is fed with dreams of wild prosperity. The girl herself is initially reluctant, finding her new suitor far too plain. 'But he's so fat!' she cries. 'Oh,' coos her conniving maid, 'that's only because he's put on weight!' Finally the whole family is bedazzled with a show of riches, and Apollo's frantic counter-offerings of music and serenades are rejected. Plutus, having achieved his triumph, reveals the whole plot and admits that he does not really want the girl at all. The family is plunged into despondency. 'But', he announces condescendingly, 'you may keep my presents.' They immediately revive and the action closes with a ballet; the French theatre still cherished its music and dance.

Le Triomphe de Plutus is interesting because, in its confrontation of two worlds, the aristocratic and the mercantile, it so closely resembles *Le Bourgeois Gentilhomme*. Its interests and sympathies, however, are completely different. Here the aristocratic world has fallen into a self-indulgent complacency. It no longer has even the dignity of its own pretensions; it is the world of Watteau and Fragonard, of swings, bouquets and blind-man's buff, a world grown so soft that it will crumble at a touch. Marivaux's play is a bitter pill in sugar coating. Most of his audience, however, would have licked away the sugar coating and never have noticed the pill. In such an age, the robustness of Molière passed as vulgarity, and had little appeal. His plays began to vanish from the repertoire, through lack of popular response or by official fiat. *Le Bourgeois Gentilhomme* was found too hearty, *Le Malade Imaginaire* too indelicate. By the end of the century, Molière's reputation was at its lowest ebb.

The end of the century also brought the Revolution. By the time it broke out, the Comédie Française had moved, yet once again, this time back to the Right Bank and the Theatre des Tuileries. (The gardens are still there, but the buildings are no more; they were destroyed in another revolution, in the nineteenth century.) The theatre was no less subject to the changes of the times than anything else. Though it had been a royalist institution, the Comédie Française was permitted to survive with a change of name, but its repertory was severely scrutinised. The law was terrifying in its generality: 'Any theatre presenting plays that are contrary to the spirit of the Revolution will be closed, and its directors arrested and subjected to the full rigour of the law.' Since royalty was now anathema, some plays were automatically proscribed. *Le Cid*, in which the monarch appears as saviour, was stricken from the company's list. Other plays were permitted after verbal changes had been made. Words smacking of the court were censored, and were replaced by others of more proletarian sympathies. *Honneur* became *humeur*; courtly honorifics gave way to *citoyen* and *citoyenne*; characters no longer spoke of being 'at court', but simply 'in Paris'. Some of Molière's plays also suffered from the tensions of the times. *Le Misanthrope* proved unacceptable because it dealt with the theme of resignation at a time when its public was demanding frantic action. But on the whole the Revolution helped to return Molière to the audience, largely because he was more than a century old, already a 'classic', and therefore safe, where newer work might find itself in political difficulties. One play in particular rose to the fore. It was, predictably, *Tartuffe*. The reasons which had made it undeservedly notorious in 1664 made it popular now. A public which could cheerfully condemn nuns to death '*à cause d'être religieuse*' welcomed a play which seemed to be, or at least could be interpreted as being, a satire on the greed and hypocrisy of the Catholic Church. Napoleon's famous comment was that if *Tartuffe* had been written during his regime he would have forbidden it. Nevertheless he allowed it to be played, and pompously complimented Mlle Mars on what seems to have been a cautiously decorous performance in the wife's role.

The Comédie Française, torn apart by dissension during the Revolution, was reunited in 1799 at yet another theatre, the Théâtre Français, close to Molière's old home at the Palais Royal. This has remained the home of the company to the present day. Originally conceived as an opera house, the Théâtre Français was the first theatre to be built on a metal skeleton and its elegant solidity reflected the reestablishment of the dramatic tradition that it housed. The nineteenth century both affirmed the place of the Comédie Française as the temple of French dramatic art, and began the restoration of Molière's reputation. We may consider the theatre first, for it is, no less than the plays, part of Molière's legacy.

For the French, the Comédie Française has always been a mixed blessing. As a government-supported institution, it has come to exemplify both the good and the ill of state intervention in the arts. Regarding itself as a living museum of its national drama, it has always found it difficult to avoid a certain custodial fussiness about its property. Since the plays were national treasures, they had to be handled with solemnity. Not merely scripts, but modes of production, were scrupulously preserved. Normally any theatre is prone to change, quick to sense and respond to shifting interests and expectations in its audience. Occasionally, however, a group cut off from the mainstream of theatrical life will preserve a style beyond its natural term. The Moscow Art Theatre on one level, and the D'Oyly Carte Opera, on another, are examples for our time, but the Comédie Française holds the record for the western world. Though high technical standards were usually insisted upon, productions, lacking fresh blood, became no longer innovative or inspired. Roles continued to be awarded by seniority, and the pall of respectability hung so heavily over the theatre that any creative impulse seemed to be stifled. At times it has seemed that the main function of the Comédie Française has been to inspire experiment and creativity, out of sheer exasperation, in others. With the Comédie championing classicism, the Romantics had to fight their way in by brute force, and the boulevard theatres found a lively public that had grown tired of the standard fare at the official house. Antoine, the apostle of naturalism in the French theatre, developed his kitchen-sink style of acting and setting largely out of a desire to be as different as possible from the Comédie where he had once walked on as an extra.

In more recent years much of this institutional pomposity has vanished, to the extent that the Comédie has seemed at times positively skittish. There was a period when it was so concerned to present a more light-hearted image that French critics began to label it '*la maison de Feydeau*' rather than '*la maison de Molière*', so full was its repertory of frothy *fin-de-siècle* farces. But a sensible equilibrium now seems to have been established between solid productions of the classics, periodically revamped, and excursions into other times and cultures, often remarkably successful. One recent venture was a production of Shakespeare's *Richard III* in a French text, with an English director imported for the occasion.

The Comédie Française is still liable to bouts of stuffiness; it is still too subject to the bureaucracy that swaddled it at birth; it is still too susceptible to political control, and to a Minister of Fine Arts whose caprices may be no less dangerous than those of Louis XIV, as members of the company have occasionally learnt to their cost. But these are all failings inherent in an institutionalised theatre. Against them must be ranged the enormous virtues. First, the Comédie Française has preserved an unbroken performance tradition of the works of its greatest period. Of the three troupes that contributed equally to the united company – the Hôtel de Bourgogne, the Marais and the Palais Royal – each contributed its particular dramatist, Racine, Corneille, and Molière, so that the works of this trinity can be traced in an undisturbed line from the *première* to the present day. Each new performance is numbered, and the archives of the Comédie preserve scrupulous records of the theatrical, as distinct from the literary history of the plays.

The Comédie Française has also preserved a standard against which other productions can be measured: an 'official' production from which more experimental work may violently depart, but which must always be seriously regarded. It has served as a mark of recognition to the talents of individual actors, and a monument to the respect paid to the art in general. It has been a model for the establishment of other national theatres elsewhere – to Great Britain, which took nearly three centuries longer to imitate it – and to Japan, whose own National Theatre responded attentively to French advice and inspiration.

Molière's works grew in prestige along with the institution to which they had contributed. Comparatively untouched by the skirmishes of the Romantic movement, which concentrated mostly on tragedy, they held attention by their own merits. Each generation has found its own Molière. *Tartuffe*, pure or adapted, has always appealed to periods critical of the Establishment. In post-revolutionary Russia it was staged as a political allegory with Tartuffe presented as an enormous figure filling and dominating the stage, while round him circulated, as on an endless treadmill, the toiling masses. The spate of *Tartuffe* revivals in our own time testifies to contemporary impatience with institutional or private hypocrisy. The Romantics rediscovered *Don Juan*, Molière's black comedy of the cynical, restless man who sees the whole world as a vehicle for the satisfaction of his desires. They also turned their attention to *Le Misanthrope*, finding in Molière's Alceste a man whose self-tormenting introspection cast him in the same mould as Goethe's Werther. In the 1920s and 30s the theatricalist movement reawakened interest in drama forms in which the actor could sustain himself without undue reliance on a literary text. This brought with it a new interest in *commedia* techniques and practices, which in turn directed attention to Molière's slighter works. Some of these have now achieved a permanent place in the repertory and the affections of audiences. *Les Fourberies de Scapin* was brilliantly revived by Louis Jouvet; subsequently, it was recreated both by the Comédie Française, with Robert Hirsch as Scapin, and by Jean-Louis Barrault playing the lead in his own muted, grey-and-brown production. Barrault brought the play to the United States on tour, and this in turn inspired a number of productions of a comedy which before had been almost completely neglected in English. *Scapin's* most recent reincarnation has been as a musical, reverting to the Italian for its title *Scapino*. Other comedies have proved adaptable to the musical form: *L'Avare* (*The Miser*) and particularly *L'Ecole des Femmes* (*School for Wives*) which has undergone a sprightly metamorphosis as *The Amorous Flea*. Such adaptations restore, though in a different idiom, the musicality and spectacle which we have seen as a major ingredient of Molière's work. They are faithful to the author's spirit, though they may depart markedly from the letter of his text.

The continuity of French tragedy in the modern theatre at large has been less secure, and less evident. Though the neo-classical formula continued to provide models for generations of less inspired dramatists, tragedy was shaken far more severely than comedy by the Romantic movement. In the early nineteenth century, the French rediscovered Shakespeare when English companies played, virtually for the first time in Paris, uncut and unadapted versions of the major plays. Shakespeare was immediately idolised by the Romantic critics, and held up as the desirable antithesis of all that the French theatre had come to stand for. Victor Hugo's enormous, sprawling tragedies, and his hardly less sprawling prefaces, show how rapidly this old/new influence worked on a theatre that had tired of its own traditions. So does Stendhal's *Racine and Shakespeare*, in which the two playwrights are compared much to the former's disadvantage. Stendhal dismisses Racinian classicism as 'the theatre of our grandparents'. He concentrates particularly on the level of formality on which these dramas were written, arguing that they evolved from a society in which 'one duke . . . even in the fondest outpourings of parental affection, never failed to address his son as "*Monsieur*"', and which was no longer acceptable, or even comprehensible, to later generations. When the turmoil was over – a battle waged sometimes with physical violence, as well as critical shafts – the works of Corneille and Racine still held their place in the repertory, though they had to move over to accommodate the newer kind of drama. On the painted ceiling of the Comédie Française the two classical tragedians and Molière have now been joined by Victor Hugo. Enshrined in the official repertoire, the tragedies have never ceased to be performed, though the company's staid, conventional productions did little to win over new adherents. More recently this has changed, under the stimulus of more experimental productions and appraisals outside the Comédie's orbit, in particular by Jean Vilar for the Théâtre Nationale Populaire. It cannot be denied, however, that for generations of French school-children Racine has meant little more than the martyrdom of the educational Thursday matinée.

In the English-speaking theatre, these problems have been multiplied by the difficult necessity of translation. This is worth considering at some length, for it involves considerations of language and metre fundamental to the original conception of the works. For classical tragedy, the favoured verse form was the rhymed Alexandrine couplet. The name probably derives from the medieval *Romance of Alexander*, for which this form was used. It rose rapidly in popularity during the Renaissance, and from 1600 to the present day has accounted for by far the greater proportion of French poetry. The Alexandrine is basically a twelve-syllable line divided by a caesura, or break, into two groups of six. Monotony is avoided by the manipulation of secondary caesurae within each six-syllable group, and a system of stress according to sense.

We might note, first, that this is a longer line than the iambic pentameter which, since the Elizabethans, has become the standard verse form for serious drama in English. This question of length is important for actors: a voice trained to a ten-syllable line may have trouble with an extra two syllables. English translators, therefore, have tended to favour their own shorter line out of tradition and convenience, and this can give problems in compressing a given amount of material into a shorter space. To take one purely mechanical, but still exasperating, problem: French tragedy, by virtue of its normal subject matter, tends to be full of classical names. The length of the French line can encompass these without strain, particularly since the language often reduces the original by a syllable or more. Augustus becomes the convenient disyllable Auguste, while Horatius compresses itself even more drastically to Horace. Neither the length of the English line, nor the English habit of preserving the original form of the names, is so accommodating. Here, for instance, is a couplet from *Britannicus* in which Agrippina offers models for Nero's conduct:

> *Qu'il choisisse, s'il veut, d'Auguste ou de Tibère;*
> *Qu'il imite, s'il peut, Germanicus mon père.*

A literal prose translation would give us: 'Let him choose, if he wishes, from Augustus or Tiberius; let him imitate, if he can, my father Germanicus.' But to squeeze these three names into two verse lines, while still trying to keep the effect of the balanced clauses (*Qu'il choisisse . . . qu'il imite*), the end rhyme, and the internal rhyme (*s'il veut . . . s'il peut*) poses horrendous problems for the translator.

The question of rhyme, however, introduces difficulties beside which the others fade into insignificance. English has never accommodated the rhymed couplet, particularly in serious drama, as easily as French – which, apart from anything else, is a highly inflected language and offers a greater range of rhyming possibilities in verb-endings. English has usually been happier with blank verse in drama, and the traditional iambic pentameter has become a highly expressive instrument, both for original work and for translations. It cannot hope, however, to reproduce the distinctive pattern that the rhymed couplet imposes on the French speech. It is a formal pattern, responsive to certain traditional practices. For instance, each line is supposed to be complete in itself. The line contains the thought. Words and phrases do not normally spill over from one line to the next. The *Britannicus* couplet quoted above is a good example.

There are of course exceptions to this rule, but they occur rarely, selectively and with an eye to a deliberate effect. *Phèdre* contains one famous example. It comes when Aricia is warning Theseus that his wife may not be all he thinks.

> *Prenez garde, seigneur: vos invincibles mains*
> *Ont de monstres sans nombre affranchi les humains;*
> *Mais tout n'est pas detruit, et vous en laissez vivre*
> *Un . . .*

'Take care, my lord; your invincible hands have freed humans from monsters without number. But all are not destroyed, and you have left alive one.' The word *un* hangs over to illustrate the thought.

Normally, the second line of the couplet contains a matching thought. Line answers line, just as rhyme answers rhyme. The effect of this is to grace the language with a sense of epigrammatic pungency, seen at its obvious best in stichomythic, or line-by-line, dialogue:

ETEOCLES *Je saurai t'épargner une chute si vaine.*
POLYNICES *Ah! ta chute, crois-moi, précédera la mienne!*
JOCASTA *Mon fils, son règne plaît.*
POLYNICES *Mais il m'est odieux.*
JOCASTA *Il a pour lui le peuple.*
POLYNICES *Et j'ai pour moi les dieux!*

In a long speech, however, the rhyme introduces a series of arbitrary closures which make it difficult to achieve the kind of crescendo that we see so richly employed in Shakespeare – in Henry V's Agincourt speech, for instance, or Lear's outcry in the storm. Phaedra's description of the progress of her infatuation can accomplish such a crescendo, because in this case the verse form is perfectly matched to the material: the desperate course of her passion is charted step by step, and each step recorded in a couplet. In other cases the wedding of form and content may be less obviously happy, and it may appear that the passion of the utterance is unduly harnessed and trammelled by the rigidity of the verse. We have suggested elsewhere that this impression is erroneous; that, on the contrary, the tensions of the play are reinforced by the subtle war between sound and sense; but there is no denying that in English the discrepancy is overwhelming. Too often the rhyme becomes a jingle, giving the impression that the translator has started at the end of the line and worked backwards. Perhaps the best way of demonstrating this is to consider, not a translation, but an example of English drama's answer to the rhymed Alexandrine, the heroic couplet. English drama, after Shakespeare, went through its own neo-classical period. This was a passing fashion only; it produced few works of lasting repute. But for a time it was all the rage, and heavily influenced by the same considerations that had produced classical tragedy in France. Here is a passage from John Dryden's *The Conquest of Granada*:

ZULEMA Hold, hold! I have enough to make me die,
But, that I may in peace resign my breath,
I must confess my crime before my death.

Mine is the guilt; the queen is innocent;
I loved her, and to compass my intent,
Used force, which Abdelmelech did prevent.
The lie my sister forged; but O! my fate
Comes on too soon, and I repent too late.
Fair queen, forgive; and let my penitence
Expiate some part of—   *Dies*

ALMAHIDE   Even thy whole offence!

This kind of language had a short life on the English stage, and for
obvious reasons. Its difficulties are patent, yet they are precisely the
same difficulties that confront the translator of Racine. He must make
an initial choice: to keep the rhyme, or abandon it. The reasons for
preserving it are substantial. In French, it is not merely decorative, nor
is it simply a metrical ornament dressing up the substance of the play.
In a very real sense, the Alexandrine couplet is the substance of the
play, a manifestation of those qualities of symmetry, contrast and
balance that, as we have seen, control the work as a whole. Thus to
sacrifice the rhyme is to sacrifice one part of the play's quality. Yet to
keep it invites awkwardness or, at the worst, absurdity. Our own
dramatic tradition, unfortunately, has taught us to associate the rhymed
couplet with burlesque, or the Christmas pantomime, rather than with
tragedy. *The Conquest of Granada*, quoted above, was the subject of a
burlesque within a few years of its birth. Some of the older translations
of French tragedy – notably Lacy Lockert's, published for years as a
'standard work', fall into this trap. The forced rhyme makes profundity
trivial, and reduces serious dialogue to a sing-song banter. More recent
translators have aimed at a compromise. Samuel Solomon, for instance,
has used rhyme selectively in his versions, often retaining it for
stichomythic dialogue, where its formal qualities accentuate the thrust
and riposte of question and answer, but restricting its use in the longer
speeches.

Molière, of course, employed rhymed couplets too. His shorter
comedies were written in prose, which offers fewer difficulties in translation – though translators might do well to remember that levels of
formality shift, and what was ordinary prose in Molière's day may
sound stilted in ours. Miles Malleson has published Molière translations, intended originally for his own performance, which rework the
French into an English vernacular. They tend to be sneered at by critics,
but are extremely able playing versions, probably truer to the author's
intent than more consciously literary renderings. But even Molière's

verse comedies present fewer difficulties than tragedy. Rhyme, even forced rhyme, is more acceptable in comedy, and modern audiences have been able to enjoy several fine versions, notably the ingenious translations by Richard Wilbur. One critic complained that Wilbur's English rhymes were too predictable. He might have noted, more fairly, that they are in Molière too – and, indeed, in Racine. Even in French the number of combinations is limited, and the same pairs recur with frequency. One knows, for instance, that *loi* will almost invariably be rhymed with *foi*. This is more than a convenient assonance. Usually, the rhymes are thematically meaningful. It is no accident that *coeur* so frequently chimes against *honneur*. Rhyme is part of the meaning of the play, and not merely a way of expressing that meaning.

A second, and related, difficulty is the choice of vocabulary. As noted earlier, the vocabulary of French tragedy in general, and of Racine in particular, is sparse by comparison with English. This sparseness derives equally from the poet's conscious choice, the dictates of classical simplicity, and the requirements of polite society. As was remarked before, there is nothing harder to translate than perfect simplicity. To reproduce it exactly in English is to invite banality. There is a classic example in *Phèdre*. Hippolytus has just listened to the outpouring of Phaedra's passion. With mounting horror, he has watched her seize his sword and try to stab herself. As she is led from the stage, Theramenes appears. He sees Hippolytus pale and shaken, without his sword, and asks what is the matter. Hippolytus replies, in French, 'Quel surpris!' To say the least, this is a masterpiece of understatement; and unless one is very careful, it comes out in English as a joke.

For this reason, translators have sometimes given up the task as impossible and devised a more ornate English that will serve Racine's ends by different technical means. A conspicuous example is Robert Lowell's *Phaedra*, a translation of a poet by a poet but, as the author insists, a 'recreation' rather than a translation. Lowell's language is more full-blooded and vigorous than Racine's. He uses words like 'guts', that the playwright and his audience would never have tolerated. He writes in new speeches. There are more metaphors in a page of Lowell than in a whole play of Racine. And yet the work is viable; it finds a counterpart for the poetic language of one culture in the poetic language of another.

Racine has been called untranslatable. The cliché is also a platitude: in the ultimate sense, everything is untranslatable. One can never render every nuance or every association from one language to another. Translation must always be a matter of compromise. The translator must determine initially, what he wants to keep and what he can afford to lose. It is Racine's peculiar difficulty that he demands a greater degree of compromise perhaps than any other dramatist except Lorca.

But translation for the theatre involves more than language. It means also evoking the mood of the society for which the play was originally composed together with the attitudes and preconceptions that the author could assume in his audience, and presenting them to another audience in another time and culture in ways that it can understand. Molière, in this respect, presents no insuperable problems. Though the values of his society have changed, they can still be assumed as the comic datum. If fathers today no longer control the lives of their sons, or choose suitable husbands for their daughters, a modern audience is still happy to accept the possibility as the mainspring of the comic action. Unfortunately, this may sometimes give the play a more frivolous character than it was intended to have; a modern audience tends to be unaware of the real power that an Arnolphe, Jourdain or Harpagon could wield. Yet Molière's comic creations have, on the whole, so much of the common nature of mankind in them that they can still speak across the centuries, and most of the plays can be revived with a minimum of changes for comprehensibility. This places the author at the opposite end of the spectrum from, say, Aristophanes, in whose comedies every other joke is an immediate topicality that has to be annotated, explained, and, in production, usually reformulated before it can amuse a modern audience. Some of Molière's comedies require a sharper sense of the contemporary social scene than others, and here directors have attempted occasional modernisations. Le Trêteau de Paris offered a modern dress production of *Les Femmes Savantes* (*The Learned Ladies*) which set the action in a twentieth-century literary gathering, rather than in a seventeenth-century *salon*; Oronte, the poet, declaimed his verse into a tape recorder. A more widely publicised production has been *Le Misanthrope* as done by the National Theatre of Great Britain. Here the action was moved forward in time to Gaulliste France. Every topical allusion was given its modern equivalent. Characters quoted contemporary newspapers and literary reviews, and were summoned not to the court but to the Elysée Palace.

Tragedy, as in other ways, is more demanding. Racine's remote, austere, courtly world has no real modern equivalent. His characters' language, actions, motivations and behaviour had little enough in common with the world of actuality when they were conceived; they have even less now, and for a modern audience to enter this decorous, structured world requires a conscious act of will that few are ready to make. Nor do these plays adapt themselves readily to the techniques and habits of the modern actor. He is trained, normally, for other things; for natural emotion, rather than for rhetoric; for conveying the pressures of the real world, rather than the nuances of the world of poetic fiction. Some attempts have been made to transpose the plays into a 'real' and more easily acceptable environment. A recent and honourable example has been the *Phèdre* produced by the National Theatre of Great Britain under the title of *Phaedra Britannica*. In this version, though the characters continued to speak in formal rhyme, the scene was shifted to India in the days of the British Raj. This allowed them to operate within the framework of a social caste-system hardly less rigid than that of France in the reign of Louis XIV, but far closer to the immediate experience of the audience. The unshakeable authority of Theseus could resume its full meaning; so could his dynamic struggle with the rival line, represented by Aricia as an Indian princess. Hindu mythology was used to approximate to the Greek divinities, with Shiva the Destroyer performing the function of Neptune in the original.

Usually, however, such adaptations tend to defeat their own purpose by a self-conscious cleverness. One thing seems to be certain, that the techniques of the realistic theatre bring little to this kind of play. Lee Strasberg, father-figure of the American 'Method' school, once told the author that he had been able to use his realistic techniques on Racine, but at one remove. He first had his actors imagine themselves as nuns and priests; then they played French tragedy. This may be the answer: not to try to bring the plays closer to the real world, but to move them even further away from it; to create a self-contained ambiance where the characters make sense in their own terms. Franco Zeffirelli attempted something of the sort in his production of a Handel opera, one of the most precious and remote of all art forms. He solved his problem by staging the work as a play within a play. The audience watched another audience, a courtly stage audience which was itself watching, behind a second proscenium, the performance of Handel. Seen at one remove, the artificiality became an acceptable convention. Similar attempts have been made to distance the audience from Racine. One production of *Phèdre* placed the characters in a pit, with the audience looking down on them as one might peer at exotic specimens in a zoo. Another framed them in mirrors, so that every move was duplicated and the characters seemed to be playing to themselves, constantly watching themselves. It was the living stage image of an introspective, shuttered drama caught in its own frozen world.

Select Bibliography

This is in no way intended as a comprehensive list. It contains some of the principal works on which I have drawn for the material in this book, together with suggestions for further reading. Some are of scholarly, some of more general interest.

CHAPTER ONE

Chamard, Henri, ed. *Le Mystère d' Adam*. Paris, 1925.
Hashin, James. 'Notes towards a reconstruction of the *Mystère des Actes des Apôtres* as presented at Bourges, 1536', *Theatre Research*, XII, no. 1, 1972.
Lebègue, Raymond. *Le Mystère des Actes des Apôtres*. Paris, 1929.

CHAPTER TWO

Cohen, Gustave. *Etudes d'histoire du Théâtre en France au Moyen-Age et à la Renaissance*. Paris, 1956.
Deierkauf-Holsboer, S. Wilma. *Le Théâtre du Marais*. 2 vols. Paris, 1954–8.
Le Théâtre de l'Hôtel de Bourgogne. 2 vols. Paris, 1968–70.
Illingworth, D. V. 'Documents inédits et nouvelles précisions sur le Théâtre de l'Hôtel de Bourgogne', *Revue d'Histoire du Théâtre*, 2, 1970–2.
Lawrenson, T. E. *The French Stage in the Seventeenth Century. A Study in the Advent of the Italian Order*. Manchester, 1957.
Lewis, W. H. *The Splendid Century: Life in the France of Louis XIV*. Garden City, 1957.
Ranum, Orest and Patricia, eds. *The Century of Louis XIV*. New York, 1972.
Roy, D. H. 'La Scène de l'Hôtel de Bourgogne', *Revue d'Histoire du Theatre*, 3, 1962.
Villiers, André. 'L'ouverture de la scène a l'Hôtel de Bourgogne', *Revue d'Histoire du Théâtre*, 2, 1970–2.
Wiley, W. L. *The Early Public Theatre in France*. Cambridge, 1960.

CHAPTER THREE

Bordonove, Georges. *Molière, génial et familier.* Paris, 1967.

Chevalley, Sylvie. 'Le "Registre d'Hubert" 1672–1673', *Revue d'Histoire du Théâtre,* 25, 1973.

Jurgens, Madeleine and Elisabeth Maxfield-Miller, *Cent Ans de Recherches sur Molière.* Paris, 1963.

La Grange, Charles Varlet de. 'Registre de la Grange', in *Archives de la Comédie Française.* Paris, 1876.

Mongredien, Georges. *La Vie quotidienne des comédiens au temps de Molière.* Paris, 1966.

Thoorens, Leon. *Le Dossier Molière.* Paris, 1964.

CHAPTER FOUR

Brereton, Geoffrey. *French Tragic Drama in the Sixteenth and Seventeenth Centuries.* London, 1973.

Turnell, Martin. *The Classical Moment.* London, 1947.

CHAPTER FIVE

Barrault, Jean-Louis. *Mise en scène de 'Phèdre' de Racine.* Paris, 1972.

Herzey, Jacques. 'Le Décor de Phèdre', *Revue d'Histoire du Théâtre,* 1, 1962.

Moore, W. G. *The Classical Drama of France.* Oxford, 1971.

CHAPTER SIX

Christout, Marie-Françoise. *Le Ballet de cour de Louis XIV, 1643–1672.* Paris, 1967.

Delmas, C. 'Le Ballet comique de la Reine (1581): structure and signification', *Revue d'Histoire du Théâtre,* 2, 1970–2.

Kirstein, Lincoln. *Dance, A Short History of Classical Theatre Dancing.* New York, 1969.

Movement and Metaphor, Four Centuries of Ballet. New York, 1970.

McGowan, Margaret M. *L'Art du ballet de cour en France 1581–1643.* Paris, 1963.

CHAPTER SEVEN

Baschet, A. *Les Comédiens italiens à la cour de France sous Charles IX, Henri III, Henri IV et Louis XIII.* Paris, 1882.

Chevalley, Sylvie. *Molière en son temps, 1622–1673.* Paris, 1973.

Duchartre, Pierre Louis. *The Italian Comedy,* trans. Randolph T. Weaver. London, 1929.

Moore, W. G. *Molière: A New Criticism.* Oxford, 1962.

Index